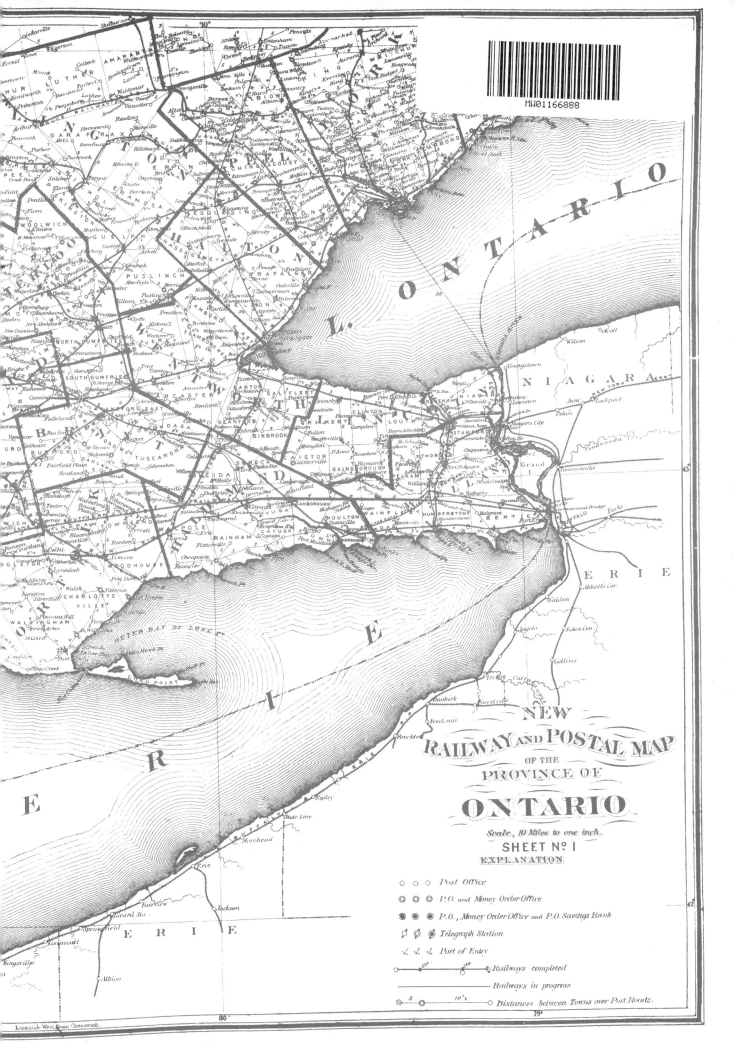

NEW
RAILWAY AND POSTAL MAP
OF THE
PROVINCE OF
ONTARIO
Scale, 10 Miles to one inch.
SHEET Nº 1
EXPLANATION

○ ○ ○ Post Office
◎ ◎ ◎ P.O. and Money Order Office
◉ ◉ ◉ P.O., Money Order Office and P.O. Savings Bank
⌀ ⌀ ◉ Telegraph Station
⚓ ⚓ ⚓ Port of Entry
●——○ Railways completed
—— Railways in progress
◎—5—●—10's—○ Distances between Towns over Post Routs.

DECOYING
ST. CLAIR TO
THE ST. LAWRENCE

Barney Crandell
11-22-88

DECOYING

ST. CLAIR TO THE ST. LAWRENCE

by
Bernard W. "Barney" Crandell
Foreword by Donal C. O'Brien Jr.

THE BOSTON MILLS PRESS

Cataloguing in Publication Data

Crandell, Barney
  Decoying: St. Clair to St. Lawrence

Bibliography: p.
ISBN 0-919783-57-0

1. Decoys (Hunting) - Ontario. 2. Decoys (Hunting)
- Michigan. 3. Wood-carving - Ontario. 4. Wood-
carving - Michigan. 5. Waterfowl in art - History.
6. Decoys (Hunting) - Collectors and collecting
- Ontario. 7. Decoys (Hunting) - Collectors and
collecting - Michigan. I. Title.

NK9713.C73 1988   745.593'09713   C88-093952-4

Published by:
THE BOSTON MILLS PRESS
132 Main Street
Erin, Ontario N0B 1T0
(519) 833-2407
FAX: (519) 833-2195

Edited by Noel Hudson
Designed by John Denison
Cover design by Gill Stead
Typography by Lexigraf, Tottenham
Printed by Tri-Graphic, Ottawa

American Association
for State and Local History
Award of Merit

Winners of the
Heritage Canada
Communications Award

We wish to acknowledge the financial assistance and encouragement of the Canada Council, the Ontario Arts Council and the Office of the Secretary of State.

CONTENTS

Foreword

Bernard W. Crandell, known to one and all as "Barney," is a great bear of an outdoorsman with the mind of a historian and the heart and soul of a poet. *Decoying: St. Clair to the St. Lawrence* has been long awaited by all of Barney's admirers and all those who love Americana and who care about the important role that waterfowl decoys play in the history of folk art.

Barney Crandell comes to waterfowl decoys from every side of the equation. He has been a duck hunter since childhood and knows how important a finely made and well-set rig of decoys are to the enjoyment and success that a gunner will derive from a day on the water. He is an imaginative and persistent scholar who has researched and written about decoys and their makers for almost two decades. His numerous articles have appeared in virtually all the relevant magazines and journals, and he has made important contributions to several books on the subject. And, last but not least, Barney has a superb collector's eye, a sense and appreciation of the beauty of decoys, and an uncanny awareness of what sets one piece apart from another and makes it truly extraordinary. This is something that very few collectors are born with and most others never attain.

Although all of these characteristics are evident in Barney's book, perhaps the most important one, and the reason why this particular chronicle is a cut above virtually every other book written on decoys, is the scholarly research which Barney brings to his subject. This is the man who unraveled the intricacies of the Mason Factory history and who came up with most of the public information on two other early Detroit commercial decoy makers, Jasper Dodge and George Peterson. This is the man who recognized the extraordinary importance of the private duck hunting clubs of the St. Clair Flats, the Detroit River and the western Lake Erie on decoy making and who, through countless hours involving travel, pursuit and interviews, wove together the wonderful tale that intertwines sportsman, maker, decoy and waterfowl. And no one tells this tale better than Barney. His style of writing is much like the man — easy and straightforward, friendly and strong, without pretense, without any hidden or personal agenda.

In short, this is a superb book written by the most qualified person that one could find from "The St. Clair Flats to the St. Lawrence," an area which arguably has produced the greatest range and the most varied type of waterfowl decoys of any area in North America.

For those of you who are not well familiar with Barney Crandell and his collection of Michigan and Ontario decoys, you are in for an exciting new journey. And for those of us who know Barney and his extraordinary collection, we can travel together on a more sentimental journey, and the best of all is that this is a journey we will now be able to take whenever the mood comes over us to spend some time with the great master and the birds he knows and loves so well.

Donal C. O'Brien, Jr.
New Canaan, Connecticut
November 10, 1987

Acknowledgements

Photography by Ron deReimacker, deReimacker Photographic, Phoenix, AZ, unless otherwise noted.

Radiography by Waterford X-Ray and Ultrasound Clinic, Pontiac, MI.

Margaret Houghton, Hamilton Public Library, for Hamilton carver research.

Ken MacPherson, Archives of Ontario, for Ontario carver research.

Julie Hall and John Castle for first reading of manuscript.

Fernlund decoys, collection of Carl Fernlund, photography by Gail Fernlund.

Taborek canvasback, Jarvis bluebill, Pomeroy redhead, Reid bluebill, unknown black, collection of James Lackenbauer. Photography of Reid bluebill, Barr canvasback by James Lackenbauer.

Gorsline decoys collection of Howard Gorsline. Photography by The Image Factory, Belleville.

Patterson whistler, "SMP" goose, photography by Bill Bresler, Livonia.

Ellis pintail, Dewar goose, Mills goose, early Schmidt geese, "T-BC" can hen, photography by Michael Hall, Bloomfield Hills.

Warin pintail, Gregory can, Mason special order whistlers, Menagh redhead/bluebill, redhead humpback, Flats lowhead redhead, hollow bluebill hen, W. Ward canvasback, Premier slope-breast black, photography by Arthur Barsamian, Birmingham.

Bach canvasback pair, collection of Ed DeNavarre.

Schweikart canvasback and whistler pair, collection of Juile Hall.

Johnston black and goose, Kelson black, collection of Russ Van Houzen.

Chambers goose color photography by Steve Story.

St. Clair Flats maps courtesy of Michael Dixon.

Introduction

Most decoy collectors have experienced the thrill of acquiring an unusually good bird and having quite an adventure in the process. We all have had a good story to tell when showing it off — "I remember very well just how and when I got that decoy!" It brings back those exciting memories again and again. This is the fun part of collecting, over and above the pleasure of looking at the treasures after they are on the shelf. I'm sure that all who have been hooked on this hobby have had experiences well worth repeating.

The author's intent in writing these few chapters has been to relate some of his rather unusual expeditions and adventures that will offer to the reader entertainment and, hopefully, some new information on old-time carvers.

A large measure of the enjoyment that has come from collecting along the St. Clair Flats and the north shores of lakes Erie and Ontario has been the companionship of my wife, Martha, and her enthusiasm in the search. Together we have built our collection. Our children, Suzanna, Jonathan and Bill (B.W.C., Jr.), also have shared in our experiences and now, as adults, enjoy decoy collecting.

Most of the decoys here are from our collection. However, we have borrowed a few from friends to help "round out" some areas. They are acknowledged on another page.

Most of the photographs show the straight side view of the decoys, which is better for analysis by collectors than the other views. I have tried to show as great a cross-section of Michigan and Ontario decoys as possible. I hope the reader will approve.

Bernard W. Crandell

An 1885 artist's bird's-eye view of the St. Clair Flats where the ship channel came into Lake St. Clair.

CHAPTER ONE: The St. Clair Flats

The St. Clair River, flowing from the south end of Lake Huron, thrusts its many channels into Lake St. Clair like a quiet hydra, its tentacles from west to east being the North Channel, Middle, South, St. Clair cutoff (shipping), Bassett, Chematogan, Johnston and Chenal Ecarte or "Sni."

Some of the islands between the channels have colorful names well known to duck hunters as well as residents: Strawberry, Dickinson, McDonald's, Sears, Harsens, Plumbush, Bassett, Squirrel, Walpole and St. Anne's, the latter four comprising an Ontario Indian reservation.

This is more than 100,000 acres of low-lying land and cattail marsh punctuated by occasional willows and thousands of ponds and potholes known as the St. Clair Flats.

An international boundary follows the South Channel through the Flats, one third of which is U.S.A., two thirds of which are Canada, and three thirds of which are mosquitoes, muskrats and ducks.

This is prime duck and goose hunting country that has attracted waterfowl hunters since the mid-1800s. In the early days they journeyed by railroad from such Canadian cities as London, Hamilton and Toronto. From the American side the Detroit area supplied the largest group of gunners.

A trip to the St. Clair Flats by Toronto hunters made news 120 or so years ago. The Toronto *Leader* of November 1860 reported: "Captain Strachan and Mr. Kennedy returned last evening from a fortnight's shooting in the St. Clair marshes, where they had excellent sport, bagging, to the two guns, two swans, three snipe, five wild geese, and 570 ducks (black, mallard and gray), weight 1,860 pounds."

The Essex *Record* of the same date also reported: "Bob Renardson has just returned with two others from a shooting expedition to Baptiste Creek. They have bagged 1,600 ducks, two bugle swans, one weighing 35 pounds and one 40, besides a variety of smaller game." Smaller game in that era included plover, rail, yellowlegs and woodcock.

Captain James McGill Strachan, an officer of the British Army, had a small houseboat in the marsh and shot there as early as 1847. His game record was in one of the early shooting books of the marsh, kept in the St. Clair Flats Shooting Company, but was lost. His diary, according to a club historian, showed that he hunted only diver ducks and that his game record for one season was 487 ducks.

Hunters from eastern Ontario generally traveled by rail to Sarnia, where the St. Clair River comes out of Lake Huron, then from Point Edwards boated downstream by small steamer the 25 miles to the Flats and the shelter of a shack or houseboat like Captain Strachan's.

So much for ancient history, geography and the mixture of people concerned.

There were many decoy makers living in the area, turning out hollow, lightweight birds that collectors now know as having the St. Clair Flats style. But many hunters brought in their own decoys from dozens of small cities and towns, and large cities like Detroit, Hamilton, Toronto, London (Ontario) and London, (England).

London, England? On a visit to the Dover marsh, on the east side of Lake St. Clair, in a period when it was being purchased by the Canadian government for a sanctuary, I looked over the few remaining decoys left by the departed club members. One of them especially struck my fancy and, after some persuasion, the manager presented to me a small, lowhead greenwing teal that he said originally had been in the rig of Peter Stroh, of brewery fame, a club member there for many years.

Dr. Miles Pirnie, Lansing, Michigan, gave this black duck wing relief and feather carving, plus a body of realistic proportions.

Rasp marks give texture to canvasback by Carl Rankin, Mitchell Bay, Ontario, Henry Ford II's Mud Creek marsh manager, c. 1945.

The teal had unusual painting, a style that seemed European in origin. So a photo was taken of it and sent to Stroh. In a reply, Stroh wrote: "I purchased it and some other teal in London on a trip in about 1955. I liked them because they were so small (10½ inches long). I could put a half dozen into a sack and carry them into the marsh with hardly any effort. They worked well, too."

The maker of the teal was a mystery until one day, while going through an early issue of Hal Sorenson's *Decoy Collector's Guide*, there it was: Austin Johnson of Colchester, England. Then the winter 1987 issue of *Wildfowl Carving and Collecting* carried an article, "Last of the English Decoy Makers," identifying the late Ted Grace of Walderslade, Kent, as the maker. In any event, the little bird had migrated a long way from home.

Also in the Dover decoy leftovers were some made by Dr. Miles Pirnie of East Lansing and Frank Schmidt of Detroit. They were to remain there, I found. But en route home I stopped at a farmhouse hard by the Dover and knocked on the door. The farmer led me to the garage, where five Pirnies poked their heads up through the debris and dust. He did not say where he had acquired the beautiful blacks and mallards, but he was not going to use them and would be glad to get them out of the way. Suffering from a colossal hangover, he snatched $50 from my hand and headed for the Half-Way House Hotel, no doubt for a quick cure.

The late Dr. Pirnie, biology professor at Michigan State University and a waterfowl expert, came very close to duplicating what a duck really looks like. The black on page 12 is a good example.

Along the shoreline north of the Dover are four notable clubs: St. Luke's, Big Point, St. Anne's and Mud Creek, the latter owned for many years by Henry Ford II.

On a visit to Mud Creek I asked the manager, the late Carl Rankin, if any old decoys remained on the premises of this 100-year-old club. "You're here a couple of years too late," he replied. "I got tired of moving those dusty old hollow decoys around from one corner of the equipment shed to another. They seemed to be in the way all the time, and we had newer ones that were better, so I took them out in the yard, piled them up and made a big bonfire of them."

After recovering my power of speech I asked Carl what decoys he was using now. Mostly Herter's balsa, he said, and many of his own. His canvasbacks were simple but stylish, solid bodies with rasp marks much like Ken Anger's (page 12), and I acquired a pair as well as an invitation to sit in Henry Ford II's clubhouse living room while downing some of his excellent Canadian beer.

Carl's brother Cliff, who managed a marsh on the Chematogan for Henry Ford II's brother William Clay Ford and Wendell Anderson, also made interesting decoys, fullbodied, along the lines of some of Tom Schroeder's, both solid and hollow, as on page 14.

Old duck-hunting clubs are an excellent source for fine old decoys, despite the Mud Creek experience. All collectors know this, and I, for one, beginning in 1965, burned a lot of gasoline both in a car and an outboard motor to contact them.

Searching the shorelines, into sheds and shanties, is an exciting and sometimes rewarding activity for the collector. Following up leads and clues is part of the fun of the hobby. Advertising for old wooden decoys is standard procedure and many times effective, but I encountered one of the most unusual ways of finding old birds only recently.

Sitting in a tavern in Mitchell Bay, munching a hamburger and awaiting the return of a person who had some decoys for me to inspect, I decided to talk decoys with the stranger sitting next to me. As soon as he learned of my interest he slipped off his stool, faced the crowded tables and, while I looked on in amazement, shouted at the top of his lungs: "Anybody got any old decoys for sale?"

Even as I cringed from such a direct frontal assault on the subject, a hand was raised at one of the tables. Sure, he had a bunch in his garage, and he was finished with duck hunting. We promptly went over to his house and into the garage.

After climbing a rickety stepladder and gaining access to the rafters (who hasn't gone through this act?) I shuffled through the dusty, puppy-toothmarked decoys. They had good utilitarian characteristics. Frank Deroevan of nearby Wallaceburg had made most of them. I took home enough for trading material and one for the shelf.

The reader is welcome to adopt this new, quick and shocking method of locating old decoys.

Full-bodied hollow canvasback by Cliff Rankin, Wallaceburg, Ontario, c. 1945.

Every collector has had, or expects to have, a "once-in-a-lifetime" find. Mine occurred with the St. Clair Flats Shooting Company, Ltd., on Bassett Island, a part of the Walpole Indian reservation. It came about this way. For many years I had stopped my boat at the club to buy the Indian fishing license for the area, offered by club manager Cliff Roy as a service to the band. When I got the decoy bug, Cliff was one of my first calls. No, he said, the club had no decoys for sale or otherwise. Absolutely no. But he offered to show me through some of the members' equipment lockers down on the canal.

Upfront in most of them were new Styrofoam or plastic decoys. But behind those and the ducks boats and other paraphernalia, sitting on dusty and untouched shelves, were the prizes, many going back to 1874, when the club was founded. Some of them, we believe, dated back to the early 1850s, as some of the members hunted the Flats under primitive conditions before the clubhouse went up.

That's as far as we could go until, on another visit, a name on one of the lockers struck me: "H J Earl." Harley Earl had been the vice-president in charge of the design staff for General Motors, and I knew him fairly well as a result of writing an article about him in the early 1950s for *Collier's* magazine.

When I called him, Earl said he would be glad to give me some of his old decoys and would leave word with Cliff to sort some out the next time he went over for a shoot. Earl died that winter, a great loss to family, friends and the industry. But when the river cleared of ice in the spring I went back to the club. Yes, Mr. Earl had left instructions, Cliff Roy said as he led the way to the lockers, trying to keep me from stepping on his heels.

He opened a locker and rummaged along the shelves as I unsuccessfully tried to edge in past his elbows for a closer look.

"Here's an old one," he said as he thrust a dirty object at me, "and here's some more." Dirt and dust obscured their features as I quickly shoved them into a gunnysack. Looking over his shoulder, I spied what appeared to be a Chambers mallard drake. Approaching the zenith of inexcusably bad manners, but too excited to care, I unashamedly requested it.

"Naw," Cliff said, trying to keep my footprints off his back, "we need that one for a model to make some more like it." I'd heard that one before and must admit that it is a nice way of saying no. This time, I really deserved it.

He locked the door after picking out what seemed to be the eight dirtiest birds in the locker and, after a short chat and many thank-yous, I got back into my 14-foot aluminum Aerocraft with my gunnysack, headed up the Bassett to the St. Clair, then up to Algonac, where I had left my car.

As soon as I hit the landing I washed the cruddy decoys and gradually exposed a Quillen hollow black, a Quillen hen pintail and mallard drake, a Mason hollow Challenge pintail hen, a lowhead Warin black and three unknowns of pleasing proportions.

It was later learned how Quillen decoys showed up so far from their home base of western Lake Erie. A number of the Pt. Mouille Shooting Club members had transferred to the St. Clair Flats Shooting Company in the 1940s, including Harry N. Torrey, Joseph B. Schulotman and Charles T. Fisher, Jr., and had taken many of their decoys with them.

Several years later, when the club decided to sell all of its old decoys, a partnership was formed with my good friend and fellow collector Judge Harry M. Seitz, Jr., of Monroe to bid on the collection. Thus we acquired several hundred duck decoys, a couple dozen geese and one swan.

The swan was originally one of seven decoys used by a hunter in the vicinity of Mitchell Bay at the turn of the century. Machine-cut nails hold them together, so I suspect they are at least 100 years old. The late Charles Bolton of Wallaceburg came across them while taking electrical wiring out of the owner's cottage and found they were for sale.

Bolton purchased two, while five found their way to the St. Clair Flats Shooting Company. Background on the swans comes from William R. Miller, regional enforcement supervisor for the Canadian Wildlife Service, who relates: "The late Cliff Roy, manager of the club, presented one such decoy to me in 1962, and later the same year I obtained one from the widow of Bolton. He had two of them in his possession for 40 years. Roy told me that two of the club's swans migrated with a member to Long Island, and two remained at the club. [One of those was taken home to Grosse Pointe by another member, Ben S. Warren.]

"Upon acquisition of my first swan I could hardly wait to get back to the motel, at which time I filled the bathtub and proved my initial surmise that there was no way the decoy could float upright unless a very heavy counterweight of some type was added. This in itself belies the fact that these decoys are hollow, I suspect even to a portion of the neck.

"I finally solved the mystery, in that the swan at the club at that time still had attached a 3¾ x 3¾ inch cast-iron plate with a flange 1¼ inch in diameter extending downward about ¾ inch. Obviously these birds were set on a cut stick that was pushed down into the marsh bottom. I feel certain that the decoy flotation was such that the bird could not have had more than two inches of water depth extending up the side of the decoy. The method of placement would allow the decoy to pivot in the wind and I suspect would greatly enhance a goose rig, especially if the swans were set along the shoreline and apart from the geese."

Although whistling swans were hunted both fall and spring on the Flats, Miller believes the decoys represented mute swans, probably copied by the carver from an old engraving in a period when artists in Europe saw only the mute swans and their sweeping curved necks.

The neck and head were made of four pieces of wood with a 10-inch spline running vertically through the sections to attach them and give them strength. Vital statistics are:

length 21½ inches, height at neck curve 17½ inches, width 10½ inches, body height 6½ inches and weight 8 pounds.

Sometime after the club's swan in original paint was purchased by another collector, I was visiting with Miller and inspected two of his swans. Both were over-painted, with some of the paint flaking off, yet they had an appeal in their antiquity, mystery of origin, construction and rarity, so I made him an offer and happily hauled the huge trophy home from Ottawa.

Since the body conformation suggested it had been made on a lathe, I had X-rays made of it, along with hollow Peterson and Dodge geese. So many construction differences showed up that I gave up the factory origin idea. Later measurements of two of the swans showed enough variations to conclude they could not have been lathe-turned from one model.

All of the St. Clair Flats Company geese and most of the ducks, as well as the swan, were in original paint — most unusual but explainable. Many of the duck decoys were divers like canvasbacks, redheads and bluebills, and had had little usage because the club members preferred pond shooting for blacks, mallards and pintails over the more strenuous open-water shooting. Many of the blacks had been repainted because of their heavy usage and some coats laced with sand to roughen the surface. The goose decoys had not been used for many years, probably because there were not enough geese going through the Walpole area to justify hunting. In the last 15 years, of course, the goose population there as elsewhere has soared.

The makers represented in this enormous flock were Tom Chambers, club manager from 1900-1942, George Warin, David Ward and John R. Wells of Toronto, John Reeves of Port Rowan, Ontario, James Weir of Hamilton, Nate Quillen of Rockwood, Michigan, and Ralph Coykendall of New York City, the latter represented by some mammoth balsa blacks and mallards.

Factory decoys included Pratt, Mason, Dodge and Peterson. There were two hollow Dodge geese and four Peterson geese, also hollow.

There were, of course, many gems among the unknowns, as well as some uglies. In the latter category were eight blacks consisting of wings and feathers taken from dead ducks and connected to a base made of a gummy, spongy, latex-like substance.

Several decoys of unknown origin could have pre-dated the founding of the club in 1874. They are hollow with center cut, not the usual St. Clair Flats style of hollowing the decoy from the bottom and sealing the cavity with a bottom board. I decided to see if X-rays would reveal anything of interest in a couple of them (pages 17 and 18).

Their ancient vintage is hinted at in the use of machine-cut nails, which were used to attach the heads to the bodies and the two body halves back together.

Machine-cut nails in various forms have been in use since about 1790, but were supplanted largely by wire nails, which entered the scene in the 1850s and became predominant in the late 1890s. With such a loose, overlapping history, it is impossible to date decoys with any degree of certainty through their nails. However, I have X-rayed enough old-time decoys to surmise that, in the areas I am familiar with, most decoys with machine-cut nails were made prior to 1870.

Those very old decoys could well have arrived on the Flats in the 1850s with the Toronto hunters, some of whose names have already been mentioned.

Another unusual feature of the club collection was the scarcity of mallard decoys. Club shooting records from the early years provide an explanation. Most of the marsh ducks were blacks, and thus the decoys were mainly of that species. Only a sack full of pintails were in the flock, several by Warin and two each by Chambers and Wells.

Chambers produced a variety of blacks, canvasbacks, bluebills and redheads, but only a few mallards. His scarce decoys, in addition to the pintails, are only two known wood ducks and one hen golden-eye. Surely there must be others still waiting to be discovered in some old boathouse, hunting shack or garage.

The club kept meticulous shooting records, and one of the officers added up the annual totals in 1974 on the club's 100th anniversary. The duck kill for 100 years totaled

Spoke-shave marks are on this hollow, center-cut bluebill believed to have been used on the Flats in the 1850s.

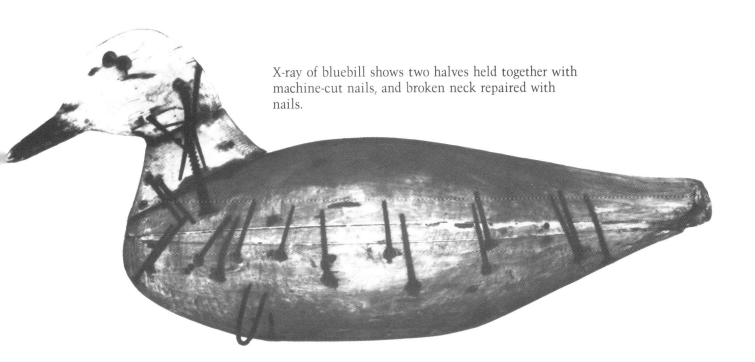

X-ray of bluebill shows two halves held together with machine-cut nails, and broken neck repaired with nails.

One of the oldest Flats decoys, c. 1850, this redhead was found at St. Clair Flats Shooting Company.

X-ray of vintage redhead shows center-cut, hollow body with machine-cut nails.

The noble high-head pose of a canvasback is caught here by Zeke McDonald, who lived on the St. Clair Flats c. 1900.

Commercial maker Frank Deroevan of Wallaceburg turned out canvasbacks like this after World War II.

The much-publicized Joe Bedore (Bedar) made this canvasback in early 1900s.

137,905. Highest annual total was 4,101 in 1882 and the lowest was 571 in 1948. George Warin held the record for most ducks in a season, 824 in 1876.

The club history frequently mentions two neighbors who became famous. We can include them here because they made decoys.

One was Christopher Columbus Smith of Algonac, who in his earlier years was a market hunter. Smith sold live decoy ducks to the club for 50 cents each, delivered messages and members to the club, tinkered with engines and boats, repaired the club's power plants and eventually founded Chris Smith & Sons Boat Company, designers and builders of the then world's fastest hydroplanes, runabouts and express cruisers bearing the Chris-Craft label.

Smith made decoys artistically with hollow, flat bodies, and on many of them screwed on a lead strip keel with his stamp, "C C SMITH." Some of the old-timers claim that Chris's brother Henry, better known as Hank, contributed to the making of many of the decoys.

The other famous neighbor was Joe Bedore, born in Quebec in 1833, who came to the St. Clair Flats and squatted on the Canadian side of the South Channel when he was about 20 years old. He loved the Flats and duck hunting and, when the Canadian government kicked him off the property, he moved across the river to the American side and established a popular hotel on Harsens Island. Attracted by his personality and stories told in his French-Canadian patois, hunters, fishermen and politicians of all types came to see Joe Bedore. He became nationally famous. No vaudeville show was complete without a Joe Bedore joke.

An old vaudeville standby had its origin in Bedore's hotel. When a customer came in and bet Joe there were four doors in the room, Joe counted the doors and covered the $5 bet. "There's the front door, the back door," Joe was told. He nodded his head in agreement. "Then there is Joe Bedore and the cuspidor." Joe could hardly wait to try the joke on a new victim, who soon appeared. "Bet you $5 there are four doors in this room," Joe offered eagerly. The wager was taken and Joe explained proudly, "There's the back door, the front door, Joe Bedore . . . and the spittoon."

For many years Joe Bedore's Bay, on the Canadian side where he originally squatted, was one of the club's shooting areas.

Joe made typical Flats-style decoys. On the bottom of his canvasbacks he branded "JOE BEDAR," which was the correct but seldom-used spelling of his name.

Across the South Channel on Harsens Island, about three miles downriver from the St. Clair Flats Company, was the Lake St. Clair Fishing and Shooting Club of Detroit, founded in 1872 by a group of Detroiters "for the improvement and perfection of marksmen." One of its early publications listed members who had joined the club prior to 1879 and it included a William James Mason, who not only was considered one of the club's best shots, but who achieved fame several decades later as founder of Mason's Decoy Factory.

The location of Mason's club, at the point where the south channel of the St. Clair River flows into Lake St. Clair, came about in a unique manner. *Outing* magazine of December 1900, in an article entitled "Sportsmen's Clubs of the Middle West," described this watery background thus:

"Sediment brought down on the current has, during the course of ages, filled the upper part of this lake, making it very shallow. Several channels break through the delta and wind their way to the deeper water below. Between these channels is marshland, grown up to rushes and wild rice. Here were ducks in abundance from the earliest times. Cadillac, the founder of Detroit, said, in 1701, that ducks covered the water so that they 'drew up in lines to let boats pass through.'

"Twenty-eight years ago three men landed from a little steamer at the building where lived the superintendent of the ship canal which the government had been obliged to cut through the shallow water at the lake's head. They hired the superintendent's son to row them to a point a few rods north of the opening of the canal, and there, in the bank of the channel, in water some six feet deep, they drove four stakes. Then followed a barge

St. Clair Flats Shooting Co. Ltd.
300 Empire Building
107 Clifford
Detroit, Michigan 48226

February 12, 1975

TO: ALL LIVING MEMBERS PAST AND PRESENT
FROM: F. James Robinson - Treasurer
SUBJECT: RECORDED DUCK KILL 1874 - 1974

Gentlemen:

I thought you might be interested in the following information which was obtained from the Club records currently in my possession:

1.   Total Kill: 137,905
2.   Highest Annual Total: 4,101 (1882)
3.   Lowest Annual Total: 571 (1948)
4.   It is interesting to note that, on June 25, 1876, Chiefs Sitting Bull and Crazy Horse, with many of their Sioux brethren, bagged 257 of the Seventh Cavalry's best, including General George A. Custer, at the Little Big Horn and, during the Fall hunting season of that same year, the Indians helped the following people bag 2,807 ducks:

NAME	OCCUPATION
Frederick Percy Austin	"Gentleman" (Ottawa)
Theodore Bright	Tea Merchant
Peter Conyer	Merchant
John Maughan, Jr.	Insurance Agent
Stephen Radcliff	Toronto City Clerk
Charles Small	"Gentleman" (Toronto)
David Ward	Pawnbroker
*George Warin	Boat Builder & Decoy Carver

5.   1974, our 100th year, yielded a total of 1,967.

It goes without saying that we who were fortunate to be members certainly enjoyed a unique place and experience and we hope that the Club with its traditions will carry on even if in a modified style.

*Holds record for ducks killed - 824 in 1876

with a pile-driver that drove great timbers into the bottom of the lake, and carpenters who built on the tops of those timbers a small frame house.

"This was the beginning of the Lake St. Clair Fishing and Shooting Club. At that time it was nine miles from the nearest land. There the members came to hunt and fish . . ."

Now called "The Old Club," its character is summer resort society and geographically, with all the land fill-ins over the years, it now rests on the south end of Harsens Island.

William Mason's early decoys were hand-carved, a canvasback (below) shows draw-shave marks in contrast to the smoothness of later lathe-made bodies. The early model also has the distinctive head carving that was copied but modified by the factory head carvers for the Premier grade.

William Mason's earliest canvasback, handmade, dates back to 1890.

William J. achieved excellence in another sport. I recall a conversation in 1972 with William Gardner Mason, then 74 years old, a nephew of Herbert W. Mason. He said William was a fine sailor, winning so many competitions on the Detroit River that when the Star Island House, a hotel, sponsored a regatta and hoped to have a new winner, Mason was politely asked not to compete.

Another family anecdote revealed that Herbert, who succeeded his father in the decoy business in the early 1900s, owned a powder magazine at the end of Holden Street in Detroit. With a contract to supply explosives to open up canals on Belle Isle, in the middle of the Detroit River, Herbert couldn't find anyone to deliver the dangerous cargo and had to haul it over in a rowboat by himself.

The northwest corner of Lake St. Clair is Anchor Bay, a vast, shallow feeding area for migrating diver ducks. The bay and the North Channel flowing into it are ringed with cities and towns, like Mt. Clemens, New Baltimore, Fair Haven, Pearl Beach and Algonac, that were well represented with decoy carvers and hunters.

Tom Schroeder sat in his second-story rooms in the Vernier Hotel in Fair Haven, exhilarated with the duck marsh environment, and whittled some of his finest pieces.

Across from the Vernier, in a small house on the waterfront, there lived Alexander "Yock" Meldrum, who made hollow canvasbacks and redheads oversize "so that ducks sitting behind a decoy would never see the approaching sneak boat."

Yock's uncle was Tobin Meldrum, another carver whose style was distinctive, with low, flat and hollow bodies, usually with a high head. He marked the underside of the bill with an "A."

Of the same generation was Henry "Budgen" Sampier of Pearl Beach. He turned out decoys featuring bills that ran to the top of the head and were sharp on the top side.

On Strawberry Island was the summer home of John Schweikart, a boatbuilder and decoy maker whose decoys had such innovative features as aluminum wing tips, fold-up keels and extra-thick necks, the latter being copied by some other Flats makers and now known as the "bull neck" style.

Of the innumerable decoys of unknown ancestry from the St. Clair Flats, these in particular deserve comment: the bluebill, whistlers and Old Squaw all on page 24. They have an unusual profile, almost like a pyramid. Of lowhead style, the heads are set approximately one third of the way back on the body and the sharp drop-off of the body front and rear offers a pyramidal pattern. They are hollow, and on two of them are strip lead original equipment keels with the imprint of Detroit lead companies. Most have been found on Harsens Island, but others have turned up on Long Point Bay. An X-ray of the bluebill shows standard construction features. The Old Squaw, incidentally, is the only one I have found on the St. Clair Flats, which hosts this species infrequently.

On the west side of Anchor Bay is Mt. Clemens, through which the Clinton River meanders en route to Lake St. Clair. Collectors are proud of the Mt. Clemens carvers, rightfully so, and Jim Kelson was the "Dean" of the Mt. Clemens school.

I never met Kelson, although I frequently passed his home near the end of the Clinton River while on fishing trips into the lake. This great hunting and fishing guide and decoy maker died in 1968 at age 79. A tribute to him by writer-outdoorsman Lee Smits highlighted the Kelson personality:

"There are so many memories of Jim, small incidents, but revealing. Anchoring a little cabin sloop beside the Kelson home, I went ashore and asked Mrs. Kelson about him. 'He's in a bad mood lately,' Cora said. 'Like today, he took out four men and here it is two in the afternoon and they haven't got their limits yet.'

"Within the hour Jim's boat docked and four jubilant clients came ashore with all the smallmouth bass the law allowed.

"A few years ago Jim underwent surgery for cataracts.

" 'The Doctor said I shouldn't read,' Jim told me. 'Mustn't watch TV. But he didn't say anything about making decoys.'

"So Jim proceeded to carve and paint 84 canvasback sleepers. He had become convinced that sleepers were far more effective than conventional decoys with straight-up necks.

"You could see, on a duck-shooting day, a decoy contest, with flocks of canvasbacks as judges. A bunch would swing into the bay, circle one spread of decoys a few times, lift and go on to the next; circle that one, flare and try another — until Jim Kelson's decoys were spotted.

"You could tell by the first swing that they liked the looks of the Kelson blocks. A few lazy circles and they'd set their wings, land among the decoys and — what is most important — stay right there while Jim and client got within easy shotgun range."

Before he turned to making canvasback and redhead sleepers from balsa, Kelson carved solid-body bluebills, blacks and mallards worthy of space on any collector's shelf.

Ancient lowhead bluebill with unusual pyramidal silhouette, maker unknown, used on Harsens Island, Lake St. Clair, by "WINSLOW" stamped on bottom.

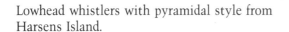

Lowhead whistlers with pyramidal style from Harsens Island.

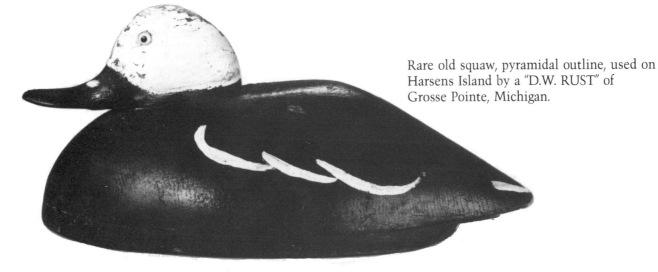

Rare old squaw, pyramidal outline, used on Harsens Island by a "D.W. RUST" of Grosse Pointe, Michigan.

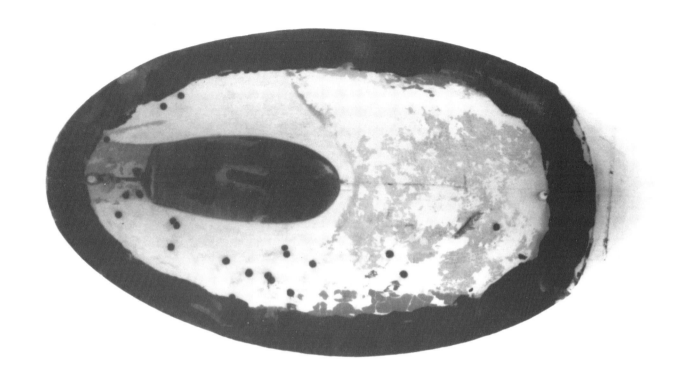

X-ray of bluebill shows two screws
holding head to body and 41 lead shot.

Those once-in-a-lifetime episodes are remarkable, but most of my acquisitions have come from a simple but straightforward system of door-knocking in a likely area. One such area was the southeast corner of Lake St. Clair, where the Thames River enters the lake at a tiny village called Lighthouse Cove, whose lighthouse serves boat traffic entering the river.

Several door-knocks finally produced Charles Mailloux, a young man who proudly led us to his boathouse to show off his decoys. The most unusual item was a hooded merganser drake. When I asked him why he had only one of them, he replied: "Well, one's all I need to attract the migs out on the lake. I try to shoot about 20 of them every fall to fill my taxidermy orders."

Charles parted with the decoy only after estimating that he had enough time left in the summer to make another one before the hunting season began.

Finding a merganser in the midwest is an unusual experience. The only other one in my collection is an American merganser hen made by the Christie brothers (Henry, Bernard, William), who moved from Detroit to Au Gres on Saginaw Bay in 1918. They made many decoys, but the mergansers are believed to be the only ones of that species ever made in Michigan.

Several more door-knocks away was Alfred Labute, a commercial fisherman whose business had been stopped for several years at least by a mercury poisoning scare. Fred had a boathouse scattered with boats, fishing gear, carpentry projects and a pile of old decoys that he no longer wanted. It was a potpourri picked up from the beach over the years. Pickings included a Mason hen pintail Premier, badly worn but still with some original paint, a Detroit-grade bluebill and a hollow bluebill hen with a "SCHWEIKART" brand on the bottom. Unlike the big Schweikarts with aluminum wing tips, its origin is a mystery, although it could have come from another member of the large Schweikart clan.

The next stop provided a good example of being somewhere too late. Yes, the manager of one of the local marshes said, he did have some nice Masons in original paint. But as I leaned forward, he quickly added, "An Illinois collector has them now." However, among the leavings were some hollow canvasbacks of enough character to be collectible, and I quickly made a deal before the competition came back for a second visit.

Up the Thames River, about two miles from Lighthouse Cove, is the famed Bradley Farms, founded by the late Bruce Bradley primarily to raise corn and beef cattle, but also to make use of the hundreds of acres of marsh for duck hunting, for a fee. I had never heard of the Bradley Farms until one Sunday in 1968, while out driving with my son Jon and his buddy Jay Shea, we stopped at a vegetable stand in Jeanette's Creek and asked where a likely place might be for finding an old duck decoy or two. The proprietor was helpful, pointing up the road toward Prairie Siding — a six-house, one-store hamlet — and "after you cross the bridge over the Thames, turn left and go as far as you can."

After following the winding road atop the Thames levee, past miles of cornfields and an occasional farmhouse, we finally drove into the Bradley compound and stopped at the first house. Two men were relaxing in the front yard and I approached them with the inevitable question. One of them was the Bradleys' marsh manager, William "Bill" Reaume, who took us into his basement to look over some decoys he wanted to sell. I purchased a Ben Schmidt canvasback hen, a Schmidt redhead, three canvasbacks from Decoys Unlimited and five unknowns of interesting appearance.

Then I asked if the Bradley Farms had any old decoys that were not being used? "Only a small barn full of them," he replied, adding that I would have to talk to John or Bob Bradley if I wanted to see them. A meeting was arranged and Bob was agreeable.

One of the most exciting moments since I began this infectious hobby came when the barn door was unlocked and we approached shelves loaded four and five deep with decoys that had been sitting there for decades with only flies, spiders and dust for company.

Climbing precariously up on a couple of boxes, my son Jon, like a monkey picking coconuts, tossed decoys down for my inspection, calling off the names of the ones he could identify: "Mason . . . Schmidt . . . another Mason . . . a Dodge black . . . here's a Mammoth-grade canvasback . . ." And so on.

There were about 14 Masons, including two Mammoths, a lowhead Premier bluebill and the remainder Detroits. Three Dodges and a Stevens black rounded out the factory ducks. Some of the gems were hollow, very lightweight, of unknown heritage. A little blue-bill (page 28) had "D S B" and "J W" brands on the bottom, and for years I have wondered if it could have been made by James Warin of Toronto, lesser-known of the two Warin brothers. His individual work has not been identified as of this date. The head of the blue-bill has Warin features, however.

Some of the "knowns" were a hollow black by Tobin Meldrum, two handsome mallard hens by Frank Schmidt, a humpback can by Roger Dolson, a hollow can and redhead by Otto Misch of Weale, near Saginaw Bay, a hollow black by Henry Sampier, and several solid-body mallards and blacks by Dimitri "Metro" Sass of Chatham. Sass made decoys for both Bradleys and the St. Luke's Club during the Depression, later becoming mayor of Chatham and owner of an iron products manufacturing plant.

One of the oddball decoys was a body with galvanized tin wings spread as in flight, but without a head.

New decoys to replace the old was the deal Bob Bradley wanted, so a couple dozen vintage ducks went home with us and Herter's oversize balsa blocks soon took their place.

Owen "Sox" Smith, one of Chris Smith's four sons, leased an area on the Chematogan Channel from the Indian band for many years. An inveterate duck hunter, Sox knew Walpole Island like the palm of his hand. More to our interest, he had a heap of old decoys resting on the rafters of one of his sheds. The birds, however, were not going to fly away as long as Sox was around.

When Smith died in 1971, the Bradleys took over the Chematogan lease. (The older generations weren't any good at spelling, either. Chematogan appeared as Chemataugha, Shewetawgan, Chimetahgun, Shewetagin, Schemetogan, Chemytaugen, Schematoghan, Chimytaugun, Shemetagun, Shewetagun, Chematogen and Chewetagen.)

After the Bradleys had moved in, son Jon and I put the 14-footer in at Algonac, revved up the 18-horsepower Evinrude and made our way across the St. Clair River to the Canadian Customs shed on Walpole, then downriver to the entrance to the Chimmy (or take any of the above spellings). A five-mile run downstream brought us to the former Smith acreage, a landmark to fishermen because it had a large barge with living quarters anchored in a cut on the shoreline.

Bob Bradley was there and, after a short discussion, the same terms prevailed on this find, too. Jon went to the rafters on a swaying, squeaky ladder and plunged into the pile, gleefully pulling out decoys with such abandon that clouds of dust, and mouse and bird manure came showering down all over me. I smiled into the storm, and tried to keep my mouth closed and eyes open as the decoy deluge started. The blocks came thumping down with such force and regularity that the "Anvil Chorus" would have been an appropriate accompaniment.

There were not as many decoys here as at Bradley Farms, but some of them made the trip a rewarding one. Most unusual of the group were six high-head, humpback canvasbacks, four drakes and two hens, about as "folk-arty" as a decoy could be. We found out later they had been made by Scott Peters, an employee of the Chris-Craft Company at the time it was manufacturing boats at the Algonac plant. Peters was a Potowatami Indian who lived on Walpole and commuted across the St. Clair River to the Algonac factory. He made decoys in the 1916-1925 period.

The unusual Peters canvasbacks went into our gunnysacks along with three Masons, several Wildfowlers and some interesting unknowns. Before calling it a day, Jon and I washed our hands, arms and faces in a nearby ditch, piled into the boat with our dirty prizes, and headed back up the channel toward Algonac, still thoroughly excited and satisfied from our successful outing.

Hollow bluebill from St. Clair Flats marked "J W," possibly James Warin's work.

Chris Smith redhead with "C C SMITH" stamped in lead strip keel has low, flat hollow body.

Lowhead redhead by Chris Smith has typically thin bottom board, c. 1910.

Lowhead black by Tom Chambers has hollow body, characteristic diamond-shaped nostrils.

Graceful black by Tom Chambers.

Tom Chambers goose has stylish lines and ⅜-inch bottom board.

Tobin Meldrum, Pearl Beach, Michigan, black has "A" carved under bill, and holes with ring of paint representing eyes.

Alexander "Yock" Meldrum made this large (15 inches long, 9½ inches high) hollow redhead for use on Anchor Bay, Lake St. Clair.

Hollow whistler by Henry "Budgen" Sampier has bill running typically almost to top of head, with sharp upper edge.

Canvasback with balsa body and fine head by Ralph Reghi of the Mt. Clemens school.

Jim Kelson of Mt. Clemens made this canvas-back sleeper with balsa body in the 1940s.

Kelson black duck with excellent wing carving and metal keel swinging downward from the rear.

Redhead from the Flats by the Christie brothers of Detroit and Au Gres, Michigan, c. 1915.

Detroit boatbuilder John Schweikart carved this distinguished canvasback with "bull" neck and aluminum wing tips, c. 1900.

"SCHWEIKART" brand is on hollow bluebill hen of unusual conformation.

Humpback canvasback, unique body contour, by Roger Dolson, Chatham, Ontario, in early 1900s.

Canvasback drake with unusual profile by Frank Dolson, Chatham, in early 1900s.

Humpback can, probably by Lester Gregory of Chatham, c. 1910.

Hollow redhead by Otto Misch of Weale, Michigan, used at Bradley Farms.

Black duck by William Finch of Port Huron has scratch painting.

Dimitri "Metro" Sass of Chatham made this deep-bodied black in 1935.

Lowhead redhead, hollow body, a common Flats style of early 1900s.

Hollow canvasback from Harsens Island, c. 1900.

Chesty lowhead redhead, maker unknown, from the Flats.

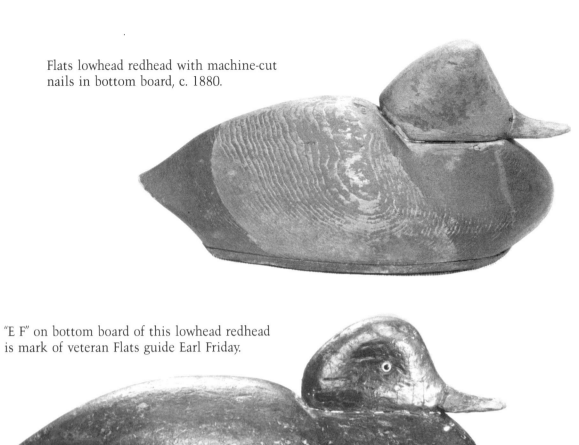

Flats lowhead redhead with machine-cut
nails in bottom board, c. 1880.

"E F" on bottom board of this lowhead redhead
is mark of veteran Flats guide Earl Friday.

This redhead is an excellent example of roughed-up
paint, a texture feature of Walter Struebing, Marine
City.

Struebing hollow canvasback is 18½ inches long, weighs 3¾ lbs.

Redhead by Garnet DeCou of Marine City, who copied Struebing painting technique.

Solid-body bluebill drake by David Simandl of Caro, Michigan, and Chatham, Ontario, who tried marketing his decoys under the "True North" stamp in 1950s.

Bluebill pair by Fred Zimmerman of Marine City and Bloomfield Hills, who copied Struebing keels but had his own excellent painting style.

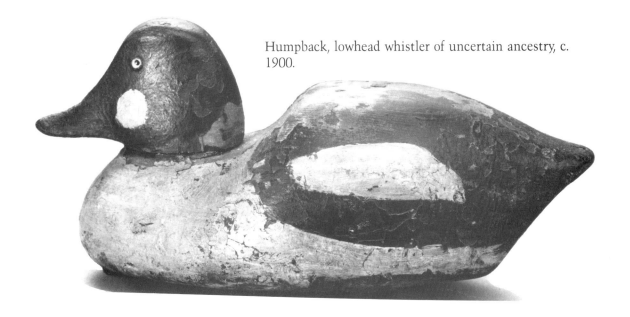

Humpback, lowhead whistler of uncertain ancestry, c. 1900.

Stylish solid-body bluebill from the St. Clair Flats Company, c. 1890.

Teddy Vandenboesch of Mt. Clemens made this fetching bobtail, preening redhead.

The "smiling" canvasbacks of Henry "Hank" Catton of Ridgetown, Ontario, have found favor on many collectors' shelves, c. 1920.

Hollow hen bluebill has appealing demeanor.

Hollow canvasback with flat body, painted eyes, from Harsens Island, c. 1910.

Hollow, very light bluebill from Harsens Island has groove cut deep in underside of bill.

Hollow pintail with tack eyes believed to have been made by John Reeves, manager, St. Clair Flats Company, c. 1890. Stamped "KENNEDY" for Reginald Kennedy, club member 1884-92.

Black with a Stevens factory profile, from Bradley Farms.

Capt. Robert Heath, New Baltimore, Michigan, made this redhead with hollow body, c. 1910.

Black with hollow body, interesting profile, Ontario origin, used by Detroit industrialist A.H. Buhl at St. Clair Flats Company.

Hollow redheads, intriguing little gems only 11½ inches long and weighing only 8½ ounces each, from the St. Clair Flats Company.

Redhead with flowing lines and hollow body, from Harsens Island.

Hollow whistler hen with typical stubby head, compact body, from St. Clair Flats.

Canvasback hen, Mt. Clemens style, has distinctive head.

Cork-body whistlers used at Mitchell Bay in the 1930s by Lew Tuller, Detroit hotel owner.

John Reeves made this stylish hollow-body goose at the St. Clair Flats Shooting Company, c. 1890.

Swimmer pose gives character to this goose found near St. Lukes on the east side of Lake St. Clair.

Goose with doweled detachable head, used at the St. Clair Flats Company by H.T. Bunbury of Hamilton, Ontario, member 1877-1901.

Hollow goose with distinctive "teeth" between mandibles, used at St. Clair Flats Company by members Francis H. Mills, 1879, then F.H. Walker, 1890.

Goose, same maker as above, has shorter neck.

Lowhead black, hollow body, from the Flats.

Lowhead black, hollow, with owner stamp "F.T.M." for
Fred Murphy, at the St. Clair Flats Company, 1924.

Beautifully contoured lowhead black used by F.H.
Walker at the St. Clair Flats Company.

Sandhill crane from southern Michigan, c.
1910.

Swan with hollow body used at the St. Clair Flats Company in early 1900s.

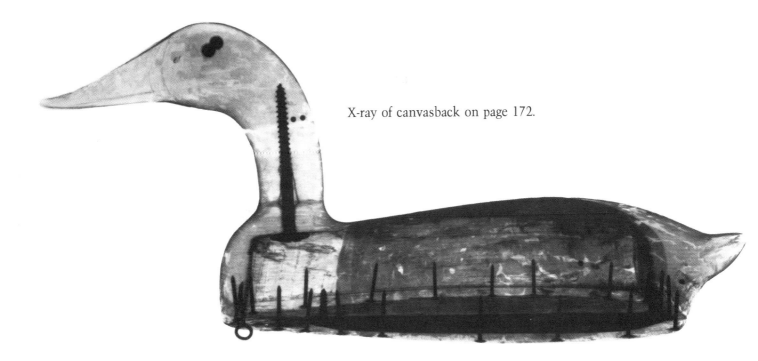

X-ray of canvasback on page 172.

Handsome full-bodied black with stamped-in feather detail by Ben Schmidt.

CHAPTER TWO: *The Detroit River*

The Detroit River, one of the busiest waterways in the world, sweeps from Lake St. Clair to Lake Erie in a huge, 32-mile arc, with the metropolitan Detroit area to the northwest and the Windsor, Ontario, environs to the southeast. For several miles of this international boundary, Ontario is *south* of U.S.A., a geographical note of dubious potential bet-making interest.

In the first half of the 20th century there were dozens of reputable Detroit-area carvers, headed by such personalities as Ferdinand Bach, Ben and Frank Schmidt, Tom Schroeder, Ralph Johnston and Charles Pozzini. Pozzini and Schroeder brought Detroit some national attention in the decoy world by winning prizes in the National Decoy Shows at the Grand Central Palace, New York City.

By far the most prolific of the carvers were the Schmidt brothers, who made decoys on a commercial scale over a span of about 40 years. The author was lucky enough to find a mallard hen sold by Ben through the J.L. Hudson Company in Detroit in the 1940s. It had been purchased by a manual training teacher for use as a model, had never been in the water, and had the purchase price on the bottom, $4.60.

Ben's decoys are of excellent proportion and painting, and they include miniatures and decoratives. He used special handmade tools for stamping in feathers, varying in size from the small feathers on the neck to the larger ones on the back of the decoy and the wings.

Frank did not put in quite as much time as Ben, as his primary concern was turning out volume. When Frank was unhurried, however, he produced some interesting examples of the decoy art, stamping in feathers with a bent wire and doing much better than a slap-it-on paint job. As a result of his prodigious production, his decoys are found everywhere within a 50-mile radius of Detroit.

Tom Schroeder is a legend in himself. He was first a cartoonist, then a Detroit advertising executive who single-handedly took on accounts he thought his creative talent could help. He helped New Era potato chips grow from a street-corner retailer into the giant of the industry. But when the first frost hit the foliage in the fall, Tom's thoughts turned to the Flats and duck hunting. He had made a few decoys now and then for his own use, but got into competitive carving after he read that Shang Wheeler of Stratford, Connecticut, made the best decoys in the world.

Having an egotistical nature, Schroeder was upset enough to go all-out producing fine decoys to challenge Wheeler, as well as anyone else entering the New York show. His blue ribbons quickly put him on the national map, and one of his construction features brought considerable comment. The Schroeder feature, wrote the Outdoor Editor of the staid New York *Times*, made the other contestants look like "rainy day whittlers." However, a head-to-head contest with Wheeler never came off, as the great Stratford carver died in 1949, the first year that Schroeder entered decoys in the show.

The Schroeder feature was "hydro-dynamics," which permitted current or wave action to flow through the bottom of the decoy, front to rear, thus stabilizing it. On some of his decoys the flow-through was achieved with a galvanized metal box approximately one inch deep, open at both ends and nailed to the bottom. On others he created a second bottom board, about one inch below the regular one and with entrance and exit holes for the flow of water. On one decoy, at least, a brant in my collection, he used only a single bottom board with entrance and exit holes cut partly into the body and partly into the board.

Whether "hydro-dynamics" sounded better than it really was, or was worth the carpentry, I do not know, as hunters who might have used Schroeder decoys and could comment on them are hard to find.

On the west side of Detroit there was a little Irishman by the name of Dannie Scriven at 100 Minnie Street — name and address worthy of Damon Runyon. Just five feet tall, but chunky, Dannie took to work every day an ash dinner basket full of rough-cut decoy heads.

"He worked at the Solvay Process plant in Delray, tending valves on steam boilers," related the late Hy Dahlka, who grew up in Trenton, not far from Dannie. "He used to sit there watching the valves and whittling with a little jackknife that had only an inch and a half of blade left. And at the end of the day he'd take all his heads, completely finished, home with him. Most were so well turned-out that only a few ever needed sanding."

Scriven (1880-1942) made mostly bluebills, redheads and canvasbacks, all of the bobtail style typical of Detroit downriver decoys. But he made more heads than decoys. Many decoy makers came to him for his fine heads, which he sold for 25 cents each. He also hunted for the market, keeping his boats at the south end of Grosse Isle.

"When Dannie died," Dahlka recalled, "six of us, all duck-hunting friends, were pallbearers. It was a dark and gloomy day, spittin' rain and blowing. I said across to one of the other pallbearers, 'If Dannie could only see what kind of great duck-shooting day it was, he'd rise up and say, "Set me down and go get 'em. Finish up with me another day."' That was just the kind of remark that witty little Irishman would have made," declared Dahlka.

Hy's uncle, William Dahlka (1894-1960) of Trenton, a carpenter, was Scriven's best customer for heads, putting them on many of the hundreds of canvasbacks, redheads and bluebills he made. He sold his decoys, all bobtail style, for $35 a dozen. He shot for the market, too, up to 1935, when market hunters were forced out of business.

One of the most prolific Detroit carvers, just a step or two behind the Schmidts, was Ralph D. Johnston, a pattern maker. Ralph had a great variety of tools at his fingertips, but the one he relied on over all the others was a band saw, which he used so expertly that most of the excess wood was off the bodies and heads by the time he picked up a knife.

From 1925-1970 Johnston made blacks and goose decoys that were outstanding, plus many other species. It is estimated that his total production was about 7,000 decoys.

One of the most unusual Michigan decoys is the sandhill crane on page 48. It appeared one day in the Port Huron Public Library, where Lowell Jackson and I were conducting a decoy exhibit and answering questions. An elderly gentleman approached us with the bird under his arm and, as it turned out, told us more about it than we could tell him.

He had obtained it from an uncle about 60 years ago, he said, and thought it had been used to decoy sandhill cranes when hunting them was allowed in Michigan. Although its shape and pose appears to be more like a bittern than a crane, I did not question the old fellow's story. He was willing to part with it and would bring it to Detroit for the big transaction. I won the coin toss with Lowell and then, one night a week later, proceeded to the sandhill crane rendezvous. The meeting place was a dark corner of the parking lot of the Detroit Police Department's Palmer Park Precinct Station on 7 Mile Road. In this unlikely location for buying decoys, I located the Port Huron car and occupant, and as the crane went into my car, the purchase price went into his. It was a staggering $20.

Picking the Canadian side of the Detroit River, with its hundreds of duck hunters, has been, for this collector at least, a disappointing experience, with one or two exceptions. Among all those hunters, one would expect to find a carver or two of note. So far, I have found only one, Frank Martin, and will leave the search for new discoveries to other collector zealots.

One point of collector interest is the Hiram Walker Distillery just a mile down-

Canvasbacks by Dannie Scriven, Detroit, c. 1920.

Ralph Johnston of Detroit put best effort into this black duck.

A "Mr. Paget" of Windsor copied a Mason Premier in carving this black.

stream from where the river leaves Lake St. Clair. (No, it's not the guided tours and the product that I'm talking about.) At least four members of the Walker family were early members of the St. Clair Flats Shooting Company, better known as the Canada Club.

The Walkers didn't miss any promotional opportunities. Some of the annual shooting summaries of the club were headed "Canadian Club," which is also the name of the Walkers' leading brand of whiskey.

Many of the club's decoys had an owner's stamp, "F.H. WALKER," after Franklin H. Walker, member from 1890-1914.

One interesting decoy found in Windsor was a hollow black by an Englishman identified only as "Paget" in the early 1920s. Paget must have liked the Mason Premier pattern, because he made a fair copy of it. The head, with carpet-tack eyes, is a close copy of Mason, if not the factory product itself, as Mason sold heads independent of complete decoys. The body is three pieces of laminated wood, plus a half-inch bottom board. The symmetry of the decoy is pleasing (above).

Farther downriver is LaSalle, a hotbed of duck hunters, who gun the islands in the river for divers and the shorelines for puddlers.

The reputable carver of LaSalle was Frank Martin, who made decoys for sale from 1925-1955. Martin's bluebills were well-made bobtail service blocks, but his blacks and mallards had some artistry in them, as on page 55. An unusual feature found on all was

Frank Martin of LaSalle, Ontario, made this large (18¾ inches long, 4¼ lbs.) black with artistic head and body.

the mandible cut which extended into the cheek almost a quarter of an inch. Martin decoys are still in use in many rigs, and the name is still spoken with reverence by many hunters who remember his carving skills.

Frank Martin put LaSalle on the decoy map, but for me LaSalle is there for another reason. On one of my door-knocking forays up and down the many canals leading into LaSalle from the Detroit River, I came across a duck hunter who admitted he hadn't been out on the flyway for a couple of years and was waiting to get up a head of steam so he'd feel like going out once more. Meanwhile, he had a stack of old decoys of all types and descriptions in his boathouse. And he could spare a few.

Up in his loft I started turning over the dozens of old decoys that were stacked five layers deep. Ah, a familiar face. Here was one that was a long way from Crisfield . . . a Ward bluebill. And another, and another.

"How did these ever get here?" I asked. The owner replied that he not only did not know but did not care. "Just bluebills to me," he said. "They work all right."

Digging deeper into the pile I found another Ward. It appeared to be painted with mallard plumage on a pintail body. This was a decoy his brother had acquired in the distant past and liked rather well. The brother, who lived next door, did indeed say the decoy was a favorite of his, but he didn't mind letting it go to a collector. A deal was consummated on the spot.

Back to the boathouse. Most of the decoys were nondescript after the unusual appearance of the Wards. But then, as I came almost to the end of the 100 or so decoys in the loft, a unique pair of canvasbacks poked out of the dust. Their high heads were mounted on round, high-domed bodies that resembled turtles (below). The bodies, probably cut from a telephone pole of large dimensions, had given the maker exactly what he wanted — something highly visible to passing flocks of canvasbacks.

The owner could offer nothing as to the origin of the "turtles" and, in all my tramping around boatsheds, I have never come across another one since. Still wondering about the Wards, I went home with them, the round jobs and a few others, an incongruous mixture, to say the least.

Solid-body, high-head canvasbacks shaped like a turtle, from LaSalle.

Of all the carvers of western Lake Erie, and even beyond, Nate Quillen (1839-1908) of Rockwood has to be rated as the perfectionist. His trades as a locksmith, cabinetmaker and boatbuilder gave him all the skills he needed for making decoys, which he proceeded to do, beginning about 1865, in his own inimitable way.

Quillen made his lowhead redheads with concave sides to the heads so that the duck hunter could easily grip them. He hollowed out not only the bodies but also the heads to achieve maximum lightness. He mortised the heads into the bodies in a rectangular recess with such a tight fit they have seldom come loose, even after 100 years of usage.

Quillen's artistic tendencies came out in the graceful, narrow necks of his regular-size birds. The necks were slim and beautiful, but couldn't stand the abuse of the marsh and were forever cracking. But they didn't fall apart. Nate thoughtfully had run a long screw up through the length of the neck to hold it together.

Quillen sold most of his decoys to members of the Point Mouillee Shooting Club, where he punted, asking $1 for the hollows and 50 cents for the solid bodies, which had knots in them, preventing hollowing. He died in 1908, but most of his decoys continued to be used by club members until the club folded in 1944.

One of the club punters, Ed Lezotte, and club superintendent Felix Zembke bought most of the members' decoys and boats. Lezotte rented out his approximately 500 decoys, most of them Masons and Quillens, at the state's boat rental concession at Point Mouille for 14 years. He stored them in a Department of Conservation garage, which caught fire in 1955 and burned to the ground, destroying everything in it.

The Zembke story has a better and somewhat humorous ending, as well as reminding collectors again to follow up a lead immediately upon hearing of it. Jim Foote, noted painter and carver, and Ed DeNavarre, collector-carver, provide the details on how the Zembke lode could have been theirs:

"In about 1966, while duck hunting, I saw a sneak boat crammed with Mason decoys in original paint, as well as some Quillens," Foote relates. "I talked to the owner, Felix Zembke, and told him that the decoys were entirely too valuable to be used for hunting.

"Felix replied that those were the only decoys he had, and so he had to use them. But that if I would like to have some, to go over to his house and pick them out.

"I said I would come over sometime, then promptly forgot about it for about a year. One day I was talking to Hy Dahlka and mentioned it to him. It should be followed up on, I told Hy."

Ed DeNavarre picks up the story, "In that period, Hy and I were doing some picking together, chasing down leads and finding an occasional good decoy or two. He mentioned the Zembke thing and we arranged a visit on a Friday to Zembke's house on the Raisin River to try to see him.

"When we got there Friday morning Zembke was gone, so we waited around all morning, hoping he would come back. At noon, being hungry, we decided to go into Monroe to eat and kill a little time. After about five hours we went back to Zembke's. Still no sign of him. We waited until dark before giving up for the day."

Dahlka called DeNavarre the next day with the bad news. He had learned that Zembke had spent the previous morning at a neighbor's house, where he could use the telephone and pass some neighborly time drinking beer. He had to use the telephone to answer an ad in the Monroe newspaper wanting old wooden duck decoys. The ad had been placed by the late Ed Childs, a leader in the Detroit-area collectors group for many years.

"I guess that Ed had collected one carload of the Zembke decoys Friday night, then made two more trips Saturday morning to finish the job," DeNavarre relates ruefully. "I just don't know how we could have missed Zembke by that close a margin."

There were between 200 and 300 decoys, DeNavarre recalls, with 18 Mason Challenge teal, 14 Mason coots, many Premiers, including a pair of pintails, all in original paint. There were also a lot of Dodges, including a widgeon, Peterson teal and five Elliston teal. And, of course, bunches of Quillens. All for about $3 each.

Dear Ed Childs, up there:
    You may now break out with your long-remembered smile!

Whistlers by Ben Schmidt have typical wing carving.

Rare bufflehead pair by Ben Schmidt.

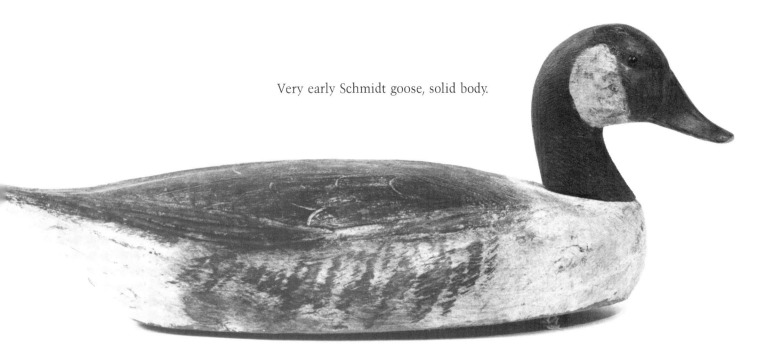

Very early Schmidt goose, solid body.

Blue goose by Ben Schmidt has hollow body with bottom board.

Canada goose by Ben Schmidt has hollow body, detachable head and neck.

Schmidt goose, an early style.

Hollow Ben Schmidt goose, beautifully contoured,
restoration by Len Carnaghi.

Goose by Earl Tomlinson, Detroit, c. 1930.

Black by Frank Schmidt has stamped-in feathering and wing outline.

Widgeon by Frank Schmidt.

Bufflehead by Frank Schmidt has typical wing indentation.

Bufflehead by Lawrence Helin of Grosse Pointe, made of laminated redwood and hollowed.

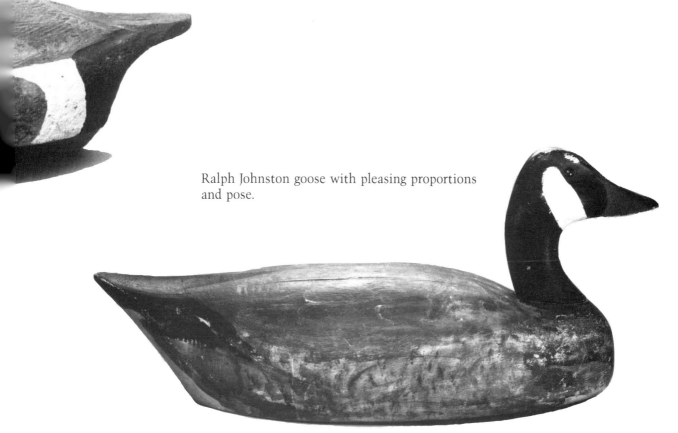

Ralph Johnston goose with pleasing proportions and pose.

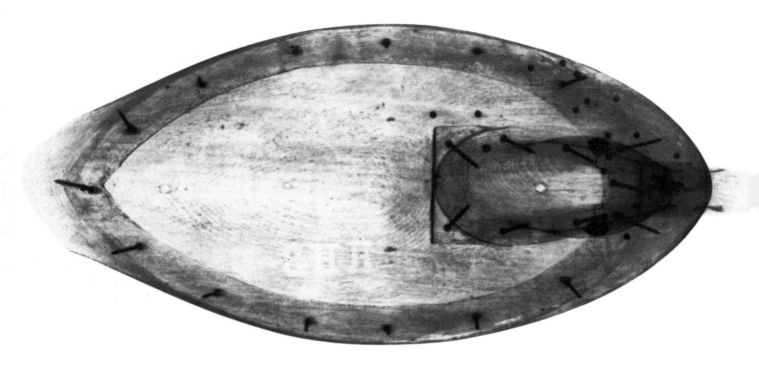

X-ray of Nate Quillen lowhead shows hollowed head, which is inletted to body.

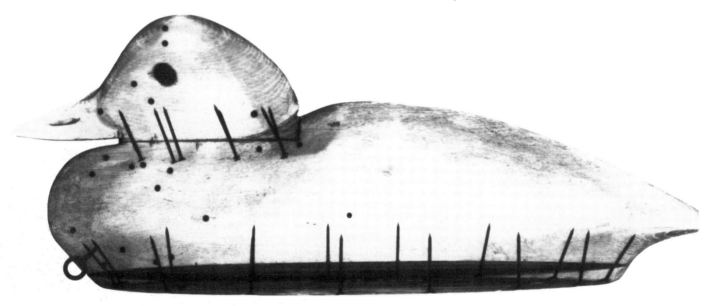

Dodge canvasback with tack eyes, dowel through head.

Dodge whistler in original paint.

Black by Dodge has feather and wing painting,
unattractive head.

Dodge bluebill with tack eyes, dowel through
head into body.

Mallard by Dodge has painted eyes.

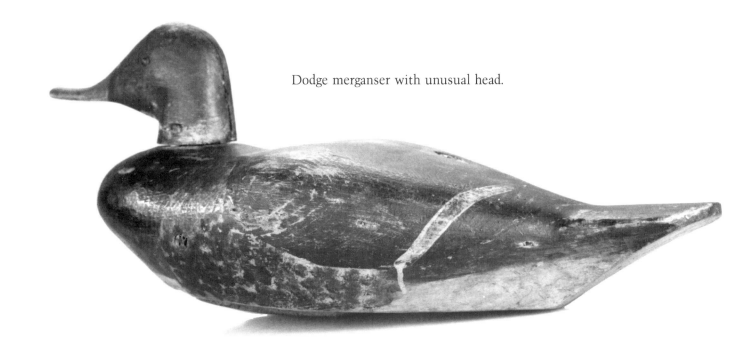

Dodge merganser with unusual head.

Peterson bluebills, unmatched pair, indicate Mason could have copied their head carving for his Challenge-grade pattern.

How many pieces in this Dodge goose? Seven. Head, neck, three in body, including bottom board, and two dowels.

Slope-breasted hollow goose believed to be work of George Peterson.

Slope-breast pintail hen, Mason Challenge.

Premier slope-breast black.

Mason special order Premier canvasback, solid body.

Snaky-head Premier canvasback.

Wood duck hen, Challenge-grade, with wing patches overpainted.

Mason Premier whistler.

Mason Premier bluebill with unusual spatulate bill.

Top view, bluebill with spatulate bill.

Premier redhead hen with different head style.

Mammoth-grade Mason canvasback hen is 19½ inches long, weighs 4⅛ lbs.

Mammoth Mason bluebill is 18 inches long, weighs 3¼ lbs.

Challenge-grade black.

Rare Premier lowhead bluebill drake is only 12¼ inches long, weighs 1⅛ lbs.

Mason Premier redheads.

Pair of hollow redheads, probably Pratt factory, with dovetailed *vertical* cut through bodies.

Close-up of Pratt redhead show-ing dovetailed *vertical* cut.

Canvasback hen with inletted head, unusual ridge-back, from Michigan.

Hollow black with extended wing primaries by Ed Murphy, River Rouge, c. 1920.

Hollow black with fine feather carving by Ed Lamerand, Rockwood, Michigan, c. 1945.

Canvasback drake with typical Detroit downriver bobtail style, by Bill Dahlka, c. 1920.

CHAPTER THREE: Long Point Bay

Curly Lounsberry revved up the 110-horsepower Johnson on his 18-foot lapstrake Thompson, warmed it enough to make it stop coughing, and slowly eased through a narrow, weed-grown channel away from his cottage on the causeway at the west end of Long Point Bay, on Lake Erie's north shore. We were headed for a rendezvous at the Bluffs Club with Jack Gleadall, club manager there for 30 years, who had told me on the telephone that he had some old duck decoys stored somewhere out near the tip of the 25-mile-long sandspit known as Long Point.

Curly, a veteran duck hunter and one of Canada's better-known trapshooters, poured the coal to the Johnson and the shoreline became a blur as we headed east, planing atop a medium chop. Shortly we came abreast of the cluster of red buildings of the Long Point Company, where Curly took on guide duties each fall during duck season.

We had stopped at the 120-year-old company on other occasions, checking up on the history of three generations of Reeves who had punted there, but this time we laid away from the club and continued on course to the northern tip of Ryerson Island. A long and shallow sandbar runs a mile out from the island, so Curly, rather than make a detour, pulled the engine up halfway and mushed through about 14 inches of water. On the other side of the bar he let things out again, and in another 15 minutes we were skimming into Bluffs Club waters.

Jack Gleadall was in the yard and waved as we pulled into a small dock. He was cleaning up the clutter left from the great storm of the previous November, 1975, and getting ready to lay the foundation for a new clubhouse to replace the 60-year-old, two-story structure washed away in the storm.

After greetings, Jack informed us that the decoys were at his cottage at Gravelly Bay, another two miles eastward, and that if Curly could pass the time at the club with one of the members, Jack would proceed with me in his square-stern canoe, taking the "inside" route that led through ponds and waterways known only to Gleadall, his guides and ducks.

It was wild, primitive marsh, and pairs of ducks flushed at every bend. Muskrats were everywhere and a lone osprey wheeled in searching circles. As we chugged toward Gravelly Bay, Jack told me that it was a small acreage known as the Anderson lease, owned by individuals who had not wanted to sell out to the Long Point Company when it made its big purchase of Crown land, nearly the entire point. Other individuals who had owned fairly large tracts, Egerton Ryerson and Dr. James M. Salmon, had deeded their land to the company for compensation and lifetime hunting rights.

Dr. Salmon's property was in fact a part of the Bluffs Club lease, and his cottage had been in use up to the day of the big storm which swept it away.

We re-entered the big bay and pulled into the shoreline at Jack's cottage. After a brief inspection of the cottage for squirrel or other damage, we went to the back of his lot, where the "garage" was located. Jack explained that at one time the south beach of Long Point could be navigated with a four-wheel-drive vehicle, and that most of the cottagers came out that way. Storms, however, had eroded the beach too much even for a FWD.

The garage was like any other equipment shed, with tools, spades, storage boxes and the like spread all over. A stack of old decoys rested in a corner and more of them lay on boards atop the rafters. I must have been transfixed by the scene, as Jack finally had to say, "Interested in any of them?" This invitation led to a response that could be compared only to the rabbit in a Walt Disney cartoon which, when surprised, leaps into the

Solid-body greenwing teal 11¼ inches long, by
Phineas Reeves.

Hen bluebills by Peter Pringle, above, and Ken Anger, below.

air and comes down with all four legs blazing. Fortunately, Jack was not standing in the path to the decoys.

They were a collection of old hollow and solid-body decoys, most in original paint, that had to be well over 100 years old. Several were branded "J.M. Salmon" and some others had the "D TISDALE" stamp, David Tisdale being one of the founders of the Long Point Company.

A little greenwing teal (page 78), appearing to be the product of Phineas Reeves, one of the original punters at Long Point Company, had the following carved into its bottom: "W.J. McC Jan'y 1913." Jack told me that was W.J. McCall of St. Williams. The teal had been repainted long ago by Jack Reeves, third-generation Long Point punter, whose painting style is easily recognized on the hundreds of repaint jobs he has done for Long Point Bay duck hunters.

A widgeon drake with solid body was a part of the next layer of decoys. Its beautiful head carving and conformation identified its creator as Charles Reeves, Jack's father, circa 1910. A stylish canvasback drake and a slope-breasted redhead drake, both "maker unknowns," came next out of the pile, then two hollow pintail drakes, also of unknown origin.

A detailed list of the 30 or so decoys on the floor and in the rafters is unnecessary, as most are illustrated here. In summary, the group was exceptionally interesting, quite collectible, and represented a cross-section of the old makers of Long Point Bay, most of the makers still unknown.

Back at the cottage, Jack served up a glass of Myers's rum with Coke, a relaxing nightcap after an exciting expedition. What was that tiny decoy on one of Jack's shelves? Something he had found on the beach, a weatherbeaten victim of storm and current . . . a cute, hollow lightweight. I added it to the three gunnysacks full of old decoys, settled up with Jack, then we started back to the Bluffs Club.

Curly was waiting patiently and helped stash the gunnysacks in his boat. We said good-bye to Jack, who was left with a mountain of work there in the yard. "What was that you said, Jack? If I want any more decoys, come over to your house in Port Rowan? A bunch of them in your barn? I'll be there, Jack, in another week."

Curly slid the Thompson away from the dock, headed it into Long Point Bay, and in a minute his big outboard was hammering homeward, pounding over two-foot waves, as the wind had been increasing throughout the day.

Long Point was unknown except to Indians until about 300 years ago, when explorers, trappers and missionaries started moving into the area. Since then, its history and that of the surrounding communities has filled with lore and legend. The point and the bay evoke images of shifting sands, storms, shipwrecks, rescues, hardwood ridges, vast marshes, ducks, muskrats, fish, the Long Point Company, Port Rowan, Turkey Point, Big Creek, poachers, rumrunners — an abundance of impressions that give this spot a mystique all of its own.

Duck hunters have come into the bay from all over the eastern half of the United States and Canada to enjoy the sport. Many Long Point Company members came from big cities like Montreal, Ottawa, Hamilton, Toronto, Boston, New York City, Chicago and even London, England.

Other clubs were the Bluffs Club, Turkey Point Club, Rice Bay Club and the Toronto Big Creek Marsh, the latter two having passed into history.

While many of the decoys of Long Point Bay were made locally, others were brought in from the outside. Ken Anger decoys, for example, show up occasionally, as well as the Nichols products from Smiths Falls, George Warin's from Toronto, and some from Hamilton. Even Nate Quillen was represented. The bay offers a fascinating mixture for the collector.

Ken Anger lived in Dunnville, about 50 miles east of Port Rowan, and so did Dunnville's other famous carver, Peter M. Pringle (1878-1953), the talented, deaf bachelor whose total decoy output of perhaps 150 birds ranks his products on the scarce scale. Anger, according to local historians, copied some of the features of Pringle decoys.

A master of the rasp, Pringle was a commercial artist and lithographer by trade, with a shop located in Toronto, and used his artistry on decoys in both paint and sculpture. His decoys have realism in their sculptural form and plumage patterns that are accurate, on most species at least, with colors blended and shaded as only a master could do.

Pringle carved from 1928-1945, using his decoys on the Grand River, from Dunnville down to Port Maitland on Lake Erie. He never sold any but did give some away. He made many different species, always using willow for the heads and either white pine or willow for the bodies.

In one phase of his carving career he numbered his decoys, stamping numerals on the bottom, from 1 to 95. Others are unnumbered, thus the uncertainty over the actual number Pringle made. On the bottom of each he gouged "P M P" in block letters 1¼ inches high. On some he also stamped a "BB" for the bluebill species, "C" for canvasback, and so on. Pringle's work is superb.

One of the many Long Point Bay "unknowns," a canvasback on page 81, has unique construction. The cut made to hollow out the body is about one fourth of the way up the body. Other features include rectangular nostrils and poured-in lead in a round one-inch hole. An X-ray of the bird (page 81) shows use of machine-cut nails and a wooden dowel attaching head to body. This decoy and some other canvasbacks and redheads of similar heritage came from the rig of Dr. J.M. Salmon, who owned property on Long Point in 1860, prior to the formation of the Long Point Company. Although I've looked, asked and X-rayed, the source of Dr. Salmon's decoys remains a mystery, as the dust of the decades has long settled over their backtrail. These were obviously not made by local talent. My guess is that they were brought in by a shooting guest from the East.

His widgeon, bluewing teal (page 190) and greenwing teal are also recluses of the realm, while his Canada goose (page 82), obtained from the president of the Bluffs Club, is also of independent origin. At least two other hollow goose decoys like this, with the unusual full-rounded tail, are in other collections.

Of the known old carvers of Long Point Bay, the best and most prolific were the three generations of Reeves. Others were Walter Bailey, Jim Smith and Isaih Brown, punters of the late 1800s. But the legions of different decoy styles found there indicate that many hands must have been busy in workshops during the winters.

The Reeves were punters for the Long Point Company. The company, formed in 1866 by a group of seven Canadian sportsmen, is an antique among duck-hunting clubs. Its original purchase of 16,000 acres from the government cost 50 cents per acre.

The company has 38 old red-painted buildings sitting on pilings over four acres of marsh and interconnected by plank walkways. It is located about halfway out on the north side of the Point and is approachable only by boat, amphibian or helicopter. Each member has his own "cottage" with some of the comforts of home, like running water, electricity, a fireplace, plus the large clubhouse with dining room.

It is not difficult to understand why this old place has been labeled "the Millionaires Club," as the roster of members past and present is replete with such names as Cabot of Boston, and the Paynes, Winthrops, Whitneys and Morgans of New York City. Canadian members of "Who's Who" status were Sir William Mulock, Sir George Drummond, Sir Hugh Allan, the Sages, Hathaways, Harrises, Ross Gooderham and Col. R.S. McLaughlin.

The original club punter was Phineas Reeves, who, with his two brothers, left Bristol, England, in the 1850s to settle in St. Williams near the bay. Phineas worked in a carriage factory as a painter, according to his grandson Jack, who died in 1987.

"My grandfather had a fine camel-hair brush he used for the fancy decorative lines painted on buggy wheel spokes and sides," Jack recounted from memories passed along by his father, Charles. "He loaded that brush up with a lot of paint so he would have enough to make one long, even line without a second dip."

Phineas later moved to Port Rowan, where he was employed as a painter at a furniture factory, doing the fine decorative trim on chairs. He and his wife, Emily, had a daughter, Jennie, and four sons, John C., Charles P., Francis, who was always known as Frank, and Henry H.

Canvasback of unknown origin from Dr. J.M. Salmon rig, c. 1860.

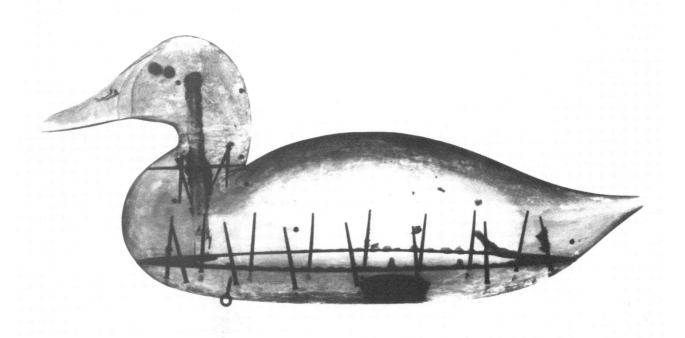

X-ray of Salmon canvasback shows use of machine-cut nails, body cut one fourth of the way up, wood dowel.

Hollow goose with owner's stamp "J.M. SALMON" on bottom.

In 1866, when the Long Point Company began operations, Phineas became the first of its punters, while son John was given the job of bookkeeper. Phineas and all of his sons except Henry made decoys. The fine brushwork that Phineas developed in embellishing buggies and chairs is readily apparent on his decoys. Wing feathers are long and flowing, and his use of colors was superb.

The styles of Phineas and John were very much alike and both used the same pattern on some decoys. On two identical mallards, for example, one is stenciled "P. REEVES" and the other "J. REEVES."

John left Long Point in the early 1890s to become head keeper of the St. Clair Flats Shooting Company. He was there only a few years before his death at the age of 36. While there, however, he made some pintail and goose decoys, the latter for Howard G. Meredith, a member in 1894, and some of these have passed on to collectors' shelves.

Frank Reeves was a punter at the Big Creek Club, at the head of Long Point Bay, for a period before guiding at Long Point Company. He made decoys with an exaggerated curve, like a new moon, to the underside of the bill.

Frank and Charles shared another unusual feature in making their decoys. They covered many of their pintails, canvasbacks and redheads with a light canvas, tacking it down tightly and then painting it. The texture of the canvas made it nonreflective in the sunlight and, according to Jack, some club members wanted this extra feature. Charles's wife, Sarah Ann, contributed a lot of her time to tacking on the canvas and folding it neatly to make it fit the body.

Charles had been the manager of the Toronto Big Creek Club for several years when son Jack was born in 1904. He then moved, as had Frank, to the Long Point Company.

Jack started helping his father make decoys when he was 16, and thus it is not surprising that their styles were somewhat alike. A prominent feature is a flatness of the upper side of the bill as it goes into the head.

Jack copied Phineas's body pattern for his mallards and blacks, almost perfectly oval-shaped. He recalls that during World War I glass eyes were impossible to obtain, so his father liberated a black bead necklace from his wife's jewelry box and used the beads for eyes. Some of the bead-eyes are still in use today.

Painted eyes, tack eyes and — most unusual of all — shoe-button eyes were also used by the Reeves. Shoe buttons were a tightly compressed cardboard with a glossy black surface, about the same size as a duck eye.

All the Reeves used cedar bodies and basswood heads. Phineas had also made some tin silhouette plover and redheads, the latter being slipped into the end of a split sapling, which then was stuck into the sandy bottom.

Jack also made cork-bodied blacks from two slabs glued together. These were so popular with a member, Junius S. Morgan, that he wanted more of them. Jack had no source for more cork, so Morgan promised to supply it. A few weeks later Jack received word that the cork had been located, but not purchased. It would have cost $8 a decoy. "Forget it," he told Jack.

Jack was the most prolific of all the Reeves, having made hundreds of decoys by his own estimate. He worked for the company for 45 years, and in addition to being its chief decoy maker, he made about a dozen skiffs for duck hunting as well. He knew John R. Wells, the famed "J.R.W." Toronto decoy maker who, with a companion known to Reeves only as Evans, shot on Long Point. Charles "Coony" Rogers, a Toronto hotel operator, was also one of their shooting companions.

On a boat ride out past the Long Point Company property, Jack pointed out a lone tree standing in the marsh. "That's where Wells and Evans had their hunting shack," he said. "Both men are long since gone and so is the shack. It was on company property, but they had a sort of 'squatter's rights' and no one bothered them."

My wife, Martha, kept a log of our next trip to Long Point. On the way home, she wrote:

"June 6, 1976. Barney and I drove to Long Point today on another one of our decoy hunting expeditions. Such a beautiful day! We followed the Lake Erie shoreline, enjoying the sparkling water and the Ontario countryside. There are many tobacco growers in this area and their unique drying barns are everywhere. We are always impressed with the neatness and obvious pride the farmers show in the care of their property.

"We went to see Jack Gleadall in Port Rowan. Here is a 70-year-old duck hunter who has been managing the Bluffs Club for the last 30 years. He had some fine old decoys in his barn which he had owned for at least 50 years. They were covered with dirt and the usual fly specks which has been my job to try to clean off. (I do believe fly droppings would make a mighty fine glue.) Several decoys had broken bills and missing eyes and are overpainted. However, most of these decoys were choice — Masons, fine old hollow birds, some made by the Reeves family. I especially liked three small widgeon, carver unknown. Five Mason Premier pintails, overpainted with a soft paint that looks like it can be taken off. And a real classic canvasback drake, hollow body and fine paint combing, initials on bottom "T-BC," "C" and "WHD." The "T-BC" was the Toronto Big Creek Club, founded in 1889 at the extreme west end of Long Point Bay where Big Creek comes in and forms a large marsh. The property is now a government wildlife sanctuary.

"There also were a bluewing teal, a greenwing teal, another widgeon drake, a hollow whistler drake and about 15 other gems, including some pintails of unknown origin. Some of the unknowns were branded "JWC," whom we had heard was J. W. Cronk, a Port Rowan merchant who was killed on a duck hunting accident on the bay. "DT" or "D. Tisdale" is on several, dating them back to the 1860s or 70s.

"We returned to Birmingham, tired but excited over our finds, wondering what they would look like when cleaned up. I've got a job to do on those fly droppings."

Hollow bufflehead found on a Long Point beach is 11 inches long, weighs 9 ounces.

Fine canvasback branded "T-BC" used at the Toronto Big Creek Club at east end of Long Point Bay.

Canvasback hen similar to the "T-BC" drake, from Capt. Bates' rig, Rondeau Bay, c. 1890.

Whistler with bold plumage pattern, ⅛-inch bottom board, bearing initials "K F" and scratched "Kurland Arcade N.Y."

Pert Whistler from rig of "JWC," J.W. Cronk, Port Rowan merchant, c. 1930.

Mallard drake with tack eyes is worthy example of Charles Reeves' work, c. 1900.

Black with hollow, oval-shaped body has interesting design by Charles Reeves.

Charles Reeves hollow pintail with shoe-button eyes.

Charles Reeves hollow canvas-back has distinctive air.

Phineas Reeves made this hollow redhead with painted eyes for David Tisdale, a founder of Long Point Company, 1866.

Phineas Reeves redhead with flat body, tack eyes.

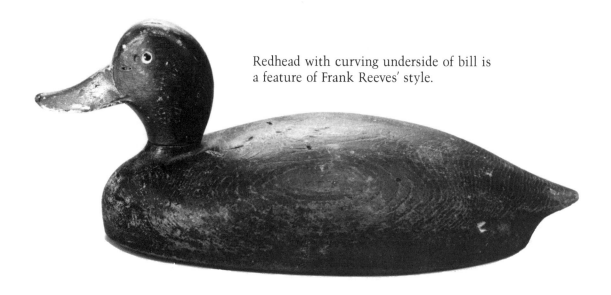

Redhead with curving underside of bill is a feature of Frank Reeves' style.

Redhead and plover tin silhouettes made by Phineas Reeves for club member Edward Harris, c. 1887. Redhead was set in water on a split sapling.

Charles Reeves canvasback is covered with canvas.

Walter Bailey of Forrestville, a punter for the Long Point Company, made this redhead.

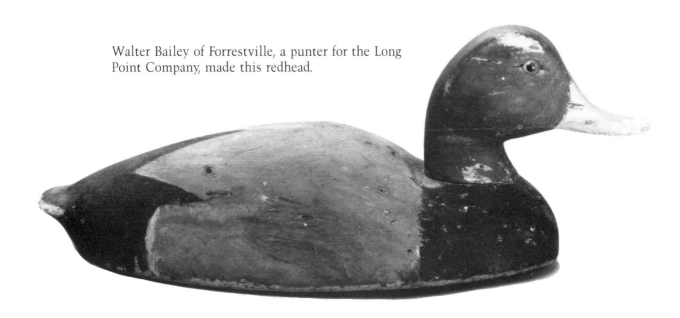

Isaih Brown, Port Rowan, carved this hollow, high-head canvasback and covered it with canvas for Long Point Company member Henry M. Sage, c. 1902.

Black duck with crazed paint from rig of J.W. Cronk of Port Rowan.

Hollow coot from Long Point Bay.

Redhead with bottom board stamped "OHP" for Oliver Hazard Payne of Cleveland, Ohio, a Long Point Company member 1898-1911.

Hollow pintail with head placed well back of breast, by Phineas Reeves, c. 1880.

Pintail with hollow body, excellent conformation, stamped "O.H. PAYNE."

Redhead pair by Davey Nichol used on Long Point Bay.

Of regal stance is this pintail with shoe-button eyes, maker unknown, c. 1880.

Oval-shaped eyes and machine-cut nails are features of this pintail used at the Bluffs Club.

Pintail used by Augustus Hemenway of Boston, a Long Point Company member 1883-1931.

Unusual flat-bodied, stubby-tailed black with tack eyes.

Hollow mallard with tack eyes, c. 1897.

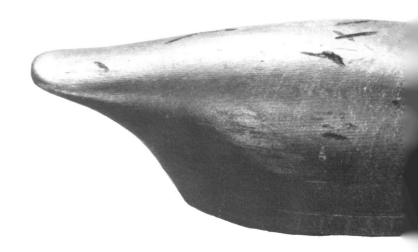

Stately black with ¼-inch bottom board. "T C KERR" and "D TISDALE" on bottom were founders of Long Point Company, 1866.

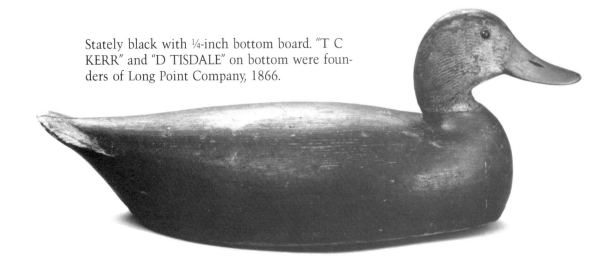

Black duck with ½-inch bottom board.

Redhead hen, hollow body with tacks set over painted eyes, c. 1866.

Hollow-body black, c. 1895.

Redhead drake with flat body and painting suggesting Reeves origin.

Redhead with tack eyes, hollow body.

Well-shaped black with shoe-button eyes, ½-inch bottom board, c. 1890.

Hollow canvasback by Phineas Reeves. "G.B.H." on bottom is George B. Harris, Long Point Company member 1877-92.

Bluebill hen, hollow lightweight with large "V" burned on bottom.

Hollow redhead with low-body profile, possibly a Reeves.

Stylish black from the J.W. Cronk rig.

High-head canvasback hen with "F.D. Smith" stencil, by Jim Smith, Port Rowan.

Hollow black from Long Point Bay.

Hollow, painted-eyes redhead with pleasing
lines, c. 1890.

Canvasback and redhead with dramatic profiles, maker unknown.

Bluewing teal hen weighing only eight ounces.

Slope-breast canvasback with interesting
contour.

Whistler drake, often called a "club head" on Long Point Bay.

Whistler hen with unusual head and bill style.

Elegant is the word for Ken Anger black duck.

Anger bluebill pair is the rasp-master's best work.

Goose by Phineas Reeves has sizable hole
routed into bottom to decrease weight.

Hollow goose by Phineas Reeves has ½-inch bottom board, excellent
painting.

Goose with upper third of body cut off to hollow out body from the top. "J.A. HEWLETT" brand was James Hewlett, New York City architect, c. 1868.

Goose of unknown origin, c. 1930.

Hollow goose with tack eyes, "J.A. HEWLETT" brand on bottom and back.

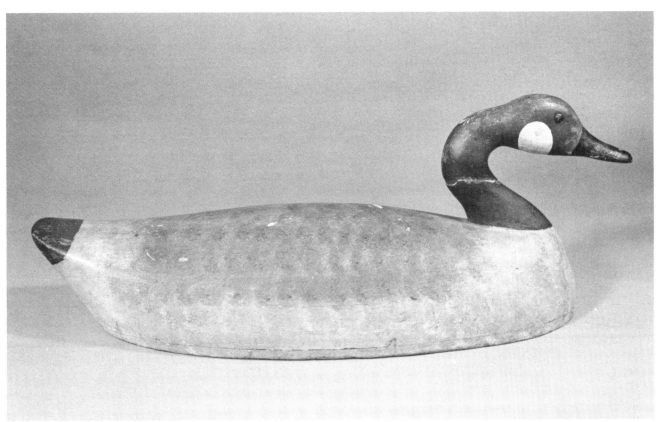

Hollow goose in aggressive pose, from St. Williams. Maker used machine-cut nails, branded "S M P" on bottom.

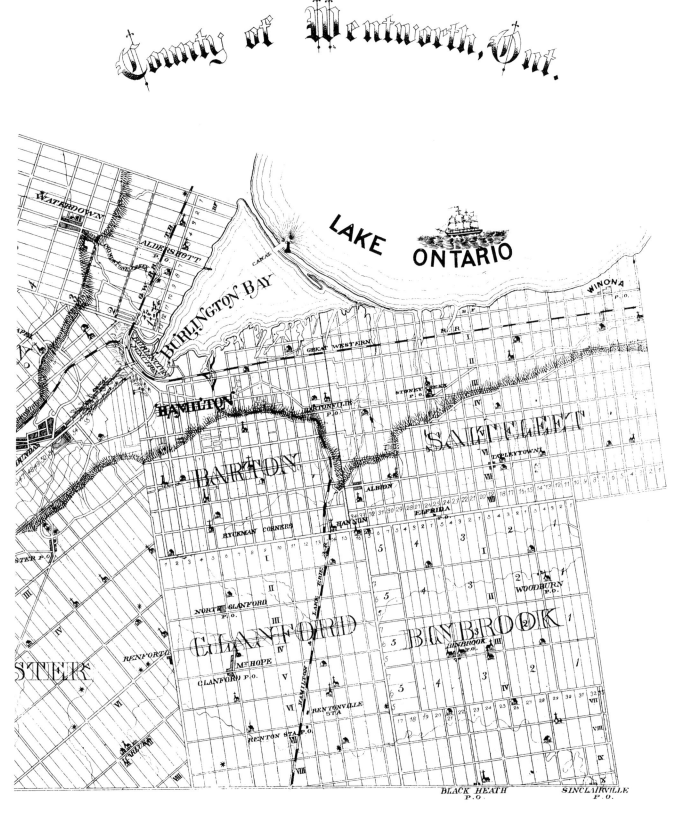

Wentworth County showing Burlington Bay from H.R. Page's Atlas of 1875.

CHAPTER FOUR: The Screeners of Burlington Bay

A century ago the Hamilton, Ontario, waterfront on Burlington Bay, at the extreme west end of Lake Ontario, was dotted with wharves, boatbuilding barns and commercial fishing sheds that represented flourishing industries. In the fall and spring, waterfowl by the thousands came into the bay to feed on the wild rice and celery, making it a duck hunter's paradise.

Burlington Bay joins the big lake via a short ship channel which cuts through a strip of shoreline known locally as The Beach. The Beach faces on Lake Ontario.

Houses and cottages on The Beach were popular domiciles for duck hunters who wanted quick access to the fine shooting. They could set up on the lake side if the wind blew from the west, or on the bay side if it blew the other way.

Many other hunters made their way to The Beach by boat or radial car, an electrically-powered old-fashioned streetcar owned by Dominion Power and Transit. The radial, its smoker reeking with ripe spittoons, ground along from Hamilton to The Beach and then to Oakville and Brantford.

The stations on The Beach where the radial stopped were numbered and were used to mark positions by the hunters, as they were spaced a quarter of a mile apart. There was a lot of competition for the positions on a first-come, first-served basis and, although the system worked pretty well, arguments and fights were not uncommon. Some hunters would have one of their sons stay all night on the beach, using only an overturned boat for shelter, to tie up a position for shooting the next morning. Station 12 was considered the best spot, as it was nearest the ship channel, over which the divers preferred flying en route to the bay, or vice versa.

Their style of hunting was called "screening." A pair of hunters would set out decoys 200 yards from the beach, the legal maximum distance from land, and wait on the shoreline for the birds to decoy. When ducks landed among the decoys, the hunters would climb into their duck boat, which had a screen of marsh grass loosely woven into a wood frame at the front end to hide them, and scull to the birds. Some hunters played out a line 170 yards long behind the boat, with one end tied to the beach. When they ran out of line they knew they were within shooting distance of the decoys.

Of all the screeners of Burlington Bay, two hunters dominated the scene.

"Harry Kretschman and George 'Red' Weir were the deadliest of all the screeners," recalled the late Ray Hazell, a retired industry executive from Hamilton. As a boy, he lived on The Beach with his father, James, a duck hunter of the early 1900s. I visited with Hazell several times before his death in 1980.

"Kretschman, the North American trap champion, was always in front with two 12-gauge Remington pumps loaded with seven shells each, the first shell having 7½ shot to use on birds on the water. Weir would shoot any ducks that went to either side.

"When they were in range, they tapped the side of the boat to make the birds go into a huddle, then would start blasting. If there were 18 ducks in the flock, almost none would get away. Kretschman was incredibly fast and accurate. The limit was 25 birds daily and they would fill before anyone else."

The pair always went to their hunting spot in Weir's launch, which he kept in a boathouse on the bay, where one of the greens of the Burlington Golf Club is now located.

Red Weir, whose father, James, founded a boatbuilding company at Hamilton in 1875, was by far the most prolific of the area carvers, turning out thousands of mostly bluebills and redheads, with a few canvasbacks and blacks, until his death in 1978 at age 94.

He was something of a character, according to Lorne Green of Mt. Hope, who as a boy had been taught to shoot by Weir.

"Red was an excellent shot, overshadowed only by Kretschman," Green recalls. "He would get so angry if he missed a shot, he would take his pump gun to a railroad track, put the barrel under a rail, and try to bend it. He called it 'straightening it out.' Then he'd throw a tin can into any water he could find nearby and pattern it. 'There, that's better,' he would say.

"Some of his barrels looked like wave action and the stocks were always chewed up from his cutting away at them. He would build them up with plastic wood. When he aimed he canted the gun to the right and kept both eyes open down over the barrel, facing more to the front. If he or Kretschman missed a shot, they figured something was wrong."

Weir made decoys for more than 50 years. On some early models he used the "J WEIR" boat company brand that went on boats. On some others he used "W.K.T." for Weir, Kretschman and George Truman, a trio that had a shack at the Old Cut on Long Point for late-season hunting. They disbanded in 1929.

Hamilton decoy carvers became a target of my curiosity in 1976, when I was attempting to identify some interesting decoys picked up at the Big Point Club, near Mitchell Bay on Lake St. Clair. One of these was a hollow bluebill (page 191), a jewel that bore "S BARKER" on its bottom board.

Samuel Barker, a railroad magnate, had been a member of Big Point before his death in 1915. His residence since 1872 had been Hamilton. I wasted a lot of time trying to find out whether Barker made decoys or just owned them, finally concluding that he was only the owner. Another decoy with the "S BARKER" stamp, found later, had quite a different style, as on page 109. In any event, my assumption is that they came from Hamilton.

The origin of some other decoys from Big Point — hollow canvasbacks and redheads — remained a mystery until one day, while visiting with Dr. Barry Wood in Oshawa, Barry showed off several recently acquired whistlers. They were from the same maker as the cans and redheads, and Barry had his name: Harry Glover of Hamilton, a bricklayer who also laid out some fine decoys in the 1920s. A trade was quickly arranged.

The Glover whistlers (page 193) have unusual heads that give the decoys a comical appearance. I flaked off several coats of old paint to reveal the original and now find the pair a never-ending source of charm and amusement. The Glover canvasback (page 193) has high-head pose plus fine combing.

Most of the Hamilton carvers made the conventional hollow decoy with bottom board and a swinging weight for the keel. However, some who had access to the pine in the Westinghouse pattern shop created elaborate decoys. Using one-inch boards, they bandsawed six pieces to make a body with cavity, laminated the three layers with glue, then reinforced the boards laterally front and rear with ¼-inch dowels. By the time other bits of wood were added for body contour, the decoy had 13 individual parts, including the head. The time-consuming carpentry involved was horrendous but, after all, the wood was free. And free of knots, too.

The boatbuilders, with their knowledge of wood and tools, were a great source for decoys. John Morris founded a boatbuilding company in 1885 at the foot of Wentworth Street, successively taken over by his son Alexander "Ek" Morris and his grandson John "Jackie" Morris. They made notable boats and decoys. One of the founder's products is on page 109, while "Ek" is represented on page 113.

Thomas Dalton and Bill Freeborn made boats and decoys from the 1870s well into the 1900s. The Weirs have already been mentioned.

Many other craftsmen in the Hamilton-Burlington area turned out artistic decoys. High on this list were Ivar Fernlund, Donny Reid, Clarence "Clary" Shaw, George "Chick" Poyton, Oscar "Oggie" Noorling, as well as Glover and Kretschman, who were mentioned earlier.

One of the most artistic and precise carvers was Ivar Fernlund, who came over from Sweden with his parents to Grand Rapids, Michigan, at age four. He worked for Westinghouse in Pittsburgh before being transferred to Hamilton in 1906 to head up the pattern shop and foundry.

Solid-body bluebill of pleasing proportions with two deep grooves under bill. Bears "S. BARKER" stamp, c. 1890.

Boatbuilder John Morris, c. 1890, made this bluebill of two pieces of wood and bottom board.

Boatbuilder Thomas Dalton made this sleek bluebill hen, c. 1880.

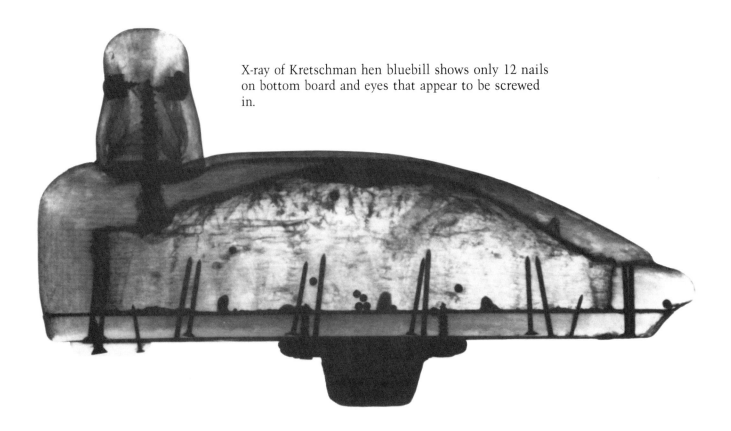

X-ray of Kretschman hen bluebill shows only 12 nails on bottom board and eyes that appear to be screwed in.

According to his son Carl, he used pattern pine for both heads and bodies, hollowing each body on a drill press with Fostner bits to an exact depth. The body shell was exactly ⅜ inch thick throughout, except for the neck area. The bottom board also was ⅜ inch.

Ivar was so exacting he made a jig to make the swinging keels. The jig held the two wires in place while the lead was poured into the mold which, of course, had an "F" on it. He even soldered the loops at the other ends of the wires for tidiness.

Fernlund lived on the beach, hunted with a model 1897 Winchester 12-gauge, made about 150 decoys of all varieties and died in 1932 at age 52.

Donny Reid, a cemetery caretaker from 1890-1920, was another screener who put an extra touch into decoys he carved for himself and for sale. He branded two "D.R." initials on the bottom board. On some decoys he carefully placed a ⅛-inch peg, or dowel, horizontally between the neck and body, apparently to keep the head from turning. The peg can easily be seen on page 192.

Thomas J. Dalton, a boatbuilder from 1868-95, turned out stylish redheads and bluebills, branding "DALTON MAKER" on many of them (page 195). For a keel he used a thin strip of ⅜-inch lead running the length of the body. Many of his decoys were used by members of the Big Point Club, while others were taken to Long Point Company by George B. Harris, club member from 1877-92. Dalton squared off the end of the bill, an unusual feature.

Kretschman, owner of the Jockey Club at the Hamilton racetrack, was as exacting in his carving as he was in shooting. His pert little hollow bluebills are only 9¼ inches long, and the half-turned head of his hen is an unusually appealing pose (page 194).

Noorling and Shaw were International Harvester employees in the 1920s. Shaw made the elaborate laminated-pattern pine bodies mentioned earlier. The wood came from his friends at Westinghouse.

Noorling made bluebills with interesting, alert heads, branding an "N" on the bottom boards (page 194).

James S. Barr carved hundreds of handsome bluebills, canvasbacks and redheads in the late 1800s and early 1900s and, like Donny Reid, placed a peg between the neck and body, visible on page 192.

Other carving notables from the Hamilton school were Rolly and brother Harry Jarvis, Ernie England, George Beattie, George Truman and Ben Taborek, a guide on Burlington Bay in the early 1930s.

The screeners of Burlington Bay have long since put away their hunting paraphernalia. Hunting on the bay declined during the 1940s due to pollution, and today only the occasional flock is seen, as the food is gone. Oil in the bay put an official stop to shooting in 1953.

The residents on The Beach now hear only the sounds of heavy traffic on Queen Elizabeth Way, a super-highway that cuts along the west end of Lake Ontario, across the ship channel leading into the bay, and down the shoreline toward Niagara. Such is progress. But some of the old-timers still around have vivid memories of how it was 60 to 70 years ago, before things changed. They'll step outside on a clear fall night, as they used to, on the chance of seeing a wedge of ducks overhead, or to test the wind to find the right shoreline to hunt. A few, at least, instead of hearing traffic on the Q.E.W., will think they hear other sounds.

Is that Red's motor launch throbbing along the bay? Is that the radial coming down the line, the motorman in his monotone calling off the stops? "Ghent's Cove . . . good luck, George . . . (that's George Beattie, who used a marsh on the bay side) . . . Gun Club . . . Tuckett's . . . Mud Bank . . . Rice Cove . . . Station 4 . . . don't shoot your foot off, Bill, or you can't kick the old lady . . . Dynes . . . Station 5 . . . Station 6 . . ." And on down the beach toward Oakville.

Hollow canvasback by William Freeborn, Hamilton, c. 1915.

George Weir bluebill with typically large head and bill.

Bluebill drake by boatbuilders Alexander "Ek" Morris and nephew John "Jackie" Morris, c. 1915.

X-ray of Morris bluebill shows wing outlines, 73 nails, 1 screw and 36 lead shot.

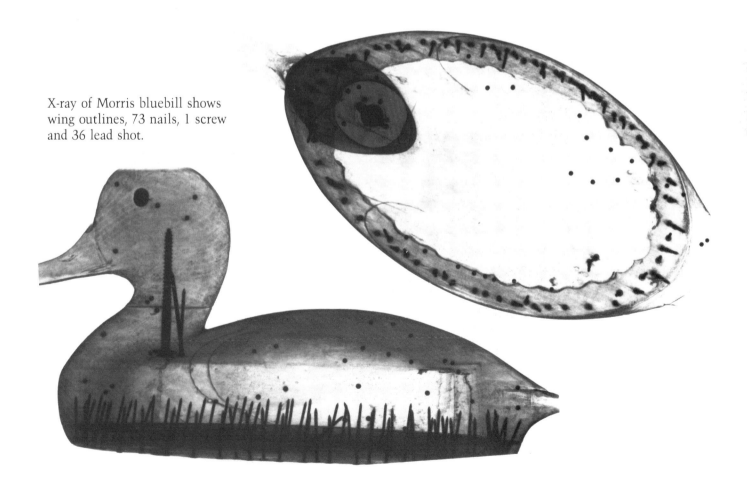

Canvasback pair by Clarence "Clary" Shaw, c. 1920.

Bluebill by Shaw copying Weir pattern.

Unfinished bluebill by Shaw shows the contrived carpentry achieved with pieces of "pattern" pine.

High-head redhead by Ernie England, c. 1930.

Perky redhead by Bill Hazell, c. 1925.

Hollow black with flat body profile, by Roland Jarvis, c. 1930.

Alert bluebill drake with flowing lines, unusual bill and nail carving.

Redhead hen, same unknown maker above, is 11½ inches long, weighs only 12 ounces.

Ben Taborek canvasback has typical swinging keel.

Roland and Harry Jarvis created this hollow bluebill.

Unknown black with tail showing Picton influence.

Hollow redhead by Ray Pomeroy of "Pomeroy Bros.," Norval, Ontario, c. 1938.

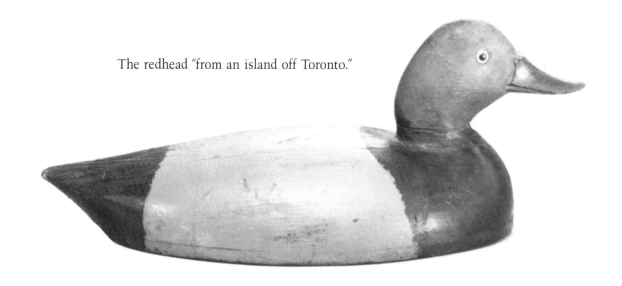

The redhead "from an island off Toronto."

Whistler, bluebill hen and black by Frank Dawson, Toronto, c. 1900.

CHAPTER FIVE: From an Island off Toronto

On a cold winter day in February 1967, fit only for skiers, ice skaters and ice fishermen, this nonenthusiast was in the village of Mitchell Bay talking to Bob Dunlop in his garage workshop. He was working on a decoy body with a draw shave but paused and laid down the blade when I finally asked him if he was selling any *old* decoys. He nodded his head and disappeared.

When Bob reappeared he was carrying a lightweight, hollow redhead (page 120), overpainted but with clean, attractive lines. There was an "X" cut on the bottom board.

"Who made it, Bob?" I asked.

"Don't know, but it came from an island off Toronto," he replied, satisfying my curiosity for the moment.

I didn't even know an island existed off Toronto. But in the following years carvers like George and James Warin, Tom Chambers, David Ward and John R. Wells came across the horizon. All from Toronto. Ward and the Warins grew up on Toronto Island before moving to the city, Ward to operate a pawnbroker business, the Warins to become boatbuilders. George had served a stint as island policeman, a job inherited from his father.

Toronto Island bends like a boomerang around Toronto's inner harbor. It was once a peninsula, until an April storm in 1858 washed a channel through its base with the mainland at the eastern end. It was inhabited by fishermen, including the Ward family, in those early years.

The center of the decoy-carving activity, however, was the Toronto waterfront in the latter half of the 19th century. It was teeming with boatbuilders, 19 separate enterprises going at one time in 1880.

George and James Warin turned out "many high-class boats," according to a story in the Toronto *Star*, as well as building the racing shell Ned Hanlon used in his five-year reign as world rowing champion. (George had taught Hanlon how to row while David Ward subsidized him as his manager.)

James Warin, before going into partnership with his brother, had worked for boatbuilder Bob Rennardson, mentioned earlier.

Frank Dawson built sailboats at the mouth of the Don River, his 33-foot sloops *Albion*, *Halcyon*, and *Seagull* well-known in the Toronto sailing fleet. He also made decoys for hunting the big lake, as well as the marshes at the south end of Lake Simcoe, with his son Arthur. His whistler, black and bluebill hen, all with hollow bodies, are on page 120.

In the late 1890s John R. "Jack" Wells was a clerk in the R.A. McCready sporting goods store, but from 1904 until 1937 worked for the boatbuilder Aykroyd Bros. on the waterfront.

Wells produced a great variety of decoys up the scale from cork-body blacks that would have a hard time making it to a collector's shelf without the "JRW MAKER" brand. His work ranged from solid-body ordinary working blocks to solid-body and hollow well-painted gems in several conformations. Some collectors don't believe he could have made them all, and I also have had some doubts.

Collector Harry Seitz, Jr., found a canvasback like the one on page 201, only with paint in such bad condition that he asked Jim Foote to repaint it for him. On the bottom board was the familiar "JRW." On others of the same grade, however, no brand appears, nor does it appear on the magnificent pair of pintails on page 201.

I took some of the questionable decoys to Jim Foote, noted carver, collector, artist and waterfowl biologist, for an opinion. He remembered well the Seitz canvasback, which he had repainted as a hen.

"You have to remember," Foote said, "that carvers selling commercially had to have several different grades of decoys to suit the various market levels. When John Wells knew he had a millionaire club hunter to satisfy, he went all out, giving his very best and then some. It is not only possible but very probable that Wells made the decoys, even though he did not brand all of them with his maker's stamp."

On that point, Wells did not even brand all of his lower-grade decoys. We will lean on Jim Foote's counsel until historians develop facts proving otherwise.

The boatbuilders possessed the tools and skills in handling wood, and it was only natural that, if they were duck hunters, they made their own decoys.

Duck hunters from other professions and occupations also made their way into decoy-carving prominence. Thomas Chambers was one of them. He was listed as a "spinner" in the 1893 Toronto directory, and a "sdlr" in 1896, working for a harness-maker. It must have been easy for Tom to leave such work for the excitement of the St. Clair Flats and the managership of two duck-hunting clubs for 47 years before retiring to his beloved Toronto and passing on to that great marsh in the sky in 1948.

George Dewar was another such emigrant. An insurance company clerk, he hunted on Toronto Island with William Ward, David's brother, until William told him in 1900 that the manager's job was open at the St. Anne's Club at Mitchell Bay, where David Ward and George Warin were members.

The St. Anne's Club, located on the Chenal Ecarte where it empties into the bay, was organized in 1876 by a group of well-to-do Canadians. The early history of the club was lost in a clubhouse fire, but one day, while door-knocking, I met George Dewar's son, Neal. I interviewed him at some length.

First of all, Dewar said, all of the old decoys like the Wards and Warins had been sold years ago in one of those "clear the decks" specials to Leo Ludenslager, a fishing and duck-hunting camp operator at Mitchell Bay, Bob Dunlop, and a Jack Grey of Sarnia. Some George Dewar decoys were among them, Neal said, as well as other Toronto carvers' products.

Every collector experiences those "too-late" moments in following up a lead, and this one has had his share, so the chance to find out where the old decoys of St. Anne's had gone immediately became a mission and a challenge, if not a crusade.

First stop, Bob Dunlop's. I had been there before, but never had any idea that he was holding a key to the repository of the lost decoys of St. Anne's.

"Where are the St. Anne's decoys?" I asked, after listening to this fine old gentleman talk for half an hour on local history and perch fishing.

He disappeared for a while, then returned with three decoys under his arms. One was a hollow canvasback of obvious antiquity with a "G W" (George Warin) burned in the bottom board (page 123). A second one, marked "D WARD," originated with one of the club's early members. The third, another hollow canvasback, was made by George Dewar (page 123), Bob said.

Asked about price, he replied with his chin thrust out a little: "I want $5 for each decoy. I've heard that a decoy has sold for as high as $25, but I just can't quite believe it."

Not being one to shake his belief, I paid the asking fee. I was so pleased to obtain the three decoys that I didn't press to find out whether that was his whole St. Anne's supply. Too bad. I found later that Dunlop hoarded them, bringing one or two out of his cache only when the mood struck him. The mood struck only if the customer listened patiently to his hunting and fishing anecdotes.

Next step on the St. Anne's trail was Ludenslager's camp. Ludenslager was a crusty character, shutting the door when he knew he had something someone else wanted. He had a shed full of old decoys and they were going to stay there. And stay there they did until he sold his camp. Fortunately, I heard about the sale shortly after it happened and went to the scene at least as fast as a Lab heading for a dead duck.

The new owner, unlike the old, was quite reasonable and did not mind at all the

George Warin canvasback with the "G.W." brand, made c. 1860.

Hollow canvasback by George Dewar, c. 1900.

idea that the shed full of birds had a cash value. My daughter, Suzanna, and I picked 14 decoys out of about 200, paid him, and went home with the prizes — a Chambers and interesting unknowns — determined to return soon to make another selection. When I did return, the situation had changed. All remaining decoys were needed that fall for the duck season.

My note on Jack Grey of Sarnia lay in a pile of other scraps of lukewarm intelligence for several years, an inexcusable and almost invariably regrettable policy. I have learned the hard way about neglecting leads, so when I finally got on the telephone to Grey I didn't expect much. I hardly expected even to find him.

"My son has those old decoys and is using them for hunting," Grey said.

Son David, a Ducks Unlimited manager in Barrie, confirmed that the old St. Anners still were in use, but with many repaints. The only one he could identify was a Warin bluebill which bore the "G & J WARIN MAKERS TORONTO" stamp. That in itself was worth the six-hour trip to Barrie.

The Warin had an in-use repaint that looked fairly good, and there were eight others whose nice lines could not be concealed by layers of paint. After taking them home, a closer examination revealed initials on the bottoms, some with both "C J M" and "W B W," and some with only "W B W." The "C J M" was probably C.J. Moore of Toronto, a founder in 1875 of the Big Point Club, which is a neighbor of St. Anne's.

The "W B W" stirred a memory flashback (which in my case is better at decoy trivia than family birthdays and such). At that moment the fun of acquiring some interesting decoys was overshadowed by the possibility of identifying another old-timer worth noting in decoy-carving history.

Eight years prior to this occasion I had made some notes on a conversation with Francis "Frank" Ward, who was living on Toronto Island. He was a grandson of William Ward, and we were speaking, of course, about decoys made by Toronto carvers of the 1860-1900 era.

"As a boy I used to watch my grandfather William make decoys for hunting here on the island and over at Lake St. Clair," Frank related. "A lot of my uncles were duck hunters, too, and some of them also made decoys."

This conversation does not establish that the "W B W" decoys were made by William Ward. If I want to believe so, however, I just have to compare their stylish bodies and perfectly round necks — an unusual feature — with those made by his brother David, and then reconstruct the background circumstances.

Since the "W B W" decoys were overpainted and my attempt to find the original layer only messed things up, I asked Ray Schalk if he could renovate one of them in the old-fashioned manner. The result is shown on page 125.

At one point in the St. Anne's search, the club manager permitted me to see the decoys currently in use. All were forgettable, with an exception: several pairs of canvasback sleepers made by "someone in Ohio." Liberating them, with new L.L. Bean decoys as replacements, I redistributed some to other collectors who know them as the "St. Anne's sleepers," as they have the St. Anne's stamp on the bottom. Several years later we discovered that the "someone in Ohio" was the late William "Bill" Enright, manager of the Erie Shooting Club, Toledo, Ohio.

Finding some of the St. Anne's old-timers was an interesting mission, but my conclusion is that a great number of the original stock is still unaccounted for, probably residing in rigs still in use in the area today.

From the observation level of the CN Tower, which at 1,185 feet is said to be the world's tallest free-standing structure, Martha and I looked out across Lake Ontario, a beautiful turquoise blue, whose surface was as scintillating as a tray full of Cartier diamonds.

We had gone to the Tower for a reason. While our first glance was out across the lake, our second was directed at the waterfront and Toronto Island, which bent in a semicircle almost below us. From our high perch we had a bird's-eye view of an important cradle of the decoy art.

Bufflehead with clean-cut lines by William Ward, c. 1890. Restored by Ray Schalk.

Redhead pair, same unknown maker from Toronto Island.

The boatbuilders along the waterfront have long since gone, and the only residents of the island now are at the east end, survivors of a battle against land-clearance campaigns by the city. Yacht clubs dot the island, a small airport sprawls at the west end, and an old lighthouse spears up from the far shore.

The island actually is a string of small islands nestled inside one long strip of land protecting them from Lake Ontario. The easternmost parcel is Ward's Island, named after the first David Ward, immigrant from Yarmouth, England, in the 1830s, who settled there as a fisherman.

I was not sure what we were going to discover up in the CN Tower at that altitude, except a feeling of dizziness, but I wanted a view of the old stamping grounds of a group of long-ago sportsmen I respect and admire. The Tower is a fitting monument to them.

Over there on Ward's Island, I pointed out, William Ward was running a small hotel in 1896 and by 1899 had left innkeeping for a job as constable. He must have been a character, as a story in the Toronto *Star* in 1905 reported the Toronto Board of Control objecting to William buying two uniforms for $40. "He never wears them," a member objected. "He goes around all the time in a white sweater and a long pair of white stockings." Ward probably didn't mind the criticism as long as he continued receiving his annual $600 salary.

Unfortunately, I have not yet found the maker of that little redhead of Bob Dunlop's "from an island off Toronto." Unfortunate, because several collectors have examples of this fine and prolific craftsman's art. The pair of redheads on page 125 and the canvasback on page 84 are from the same maker.

The redheads were used at least 70 years ago on the Humber River, which cuts through the western part of metropolitan Toronto before emptying into Humber Bay, just west of the island.

The black duck (page 47) is by the same maker. On the underside of all the bills, the carver's whittling has not been smoothed down, leaving irregular knife marks. The maker's use of wire nails on the bottom boards would, I suppose, place their date of origin in the late 1800s or early 1900s.

Down there, somewhere, I said, the "unknown" labored. Could he have been another of the Wards? Or a "Sam Beatty," mentioned by Frank Ward as a Toronto Island decoy maker? Or possibly Edward Durnan or his son John, both ardent duck hunters, who owned a boat livery at the west end of the island? Or, are these fine decoys possibly the product of James Warin, who could have been making decoys before going into partnership with his brother George? Other collectors may yet develop clues to sort it all out.

And over there on the west end is where the master decoy artist George Warin spent the later years of his life. The area is called Hanlon's Point, renamed in honor of Ned Hanlon after his rowing exploits.

Warin, one of Canada's leading sportsmen despite having lost his left arm from a gunshot wound, traveled the western provinces occasionally when not at his favorite club on the St. Clair Flats. A newspaper picture of Warin, David Ward and some other hunting buddies posing in front of a tremendous bag of ducks, geese and swans during a Manitoba trip, shows him full-bearded and with his 4-bore held in his good right arm.

A large number of Toronto decoys have shown up in Manitoba, probably left there by Warin and his companions on that trip or on others, like the one in 1901 when he guided the Duke of York, later George V, at the delta marsh.

When Warin died on July 24, 1905, funeral services were held at his residence on Hanlon's Point. "Afterward," reported the Toronto *Telegram*, "the remains were placed on the steamer *Luella*, which also brought the mourners and friends to the city at Bay Street wharf, where a funeral procession was formed to the St. James Cemetery, many well-known sportsmen and old citizens being noticed in line."

George's last trip, Martha said, was in a boat crossing his beloved bay.

Hollow goose with shoe-button eyes by George Dewar, late 1800s.

William Ward canvasback, candidate for any collector's shelf.

Lowhead black, hollow body, by David Ward, c. 1880.

Canvasback pair by David Ward with typically Ward round necks.

Black duck with simple, appealing lines, by Cliff Avvan, Toronto.

Later model Warin canvasback with shorter body and brand "G & J WARIN BUILDERS TORONTO."

Solid-body bluebill by George Warin.

Warin bluebill with high body, good paint combing, branded "G & J WARIN MAKERS TORONTO."

Warin bluebill with smaller, lower body.

Hollow redhead with Warin stamp and owner's name "W.A. ALLAN," member St. Clair Flats Company 1876.

Solid-body Warin redhead has beautiful head with painted black line along junction of bill and head, and along lower edge of bill.

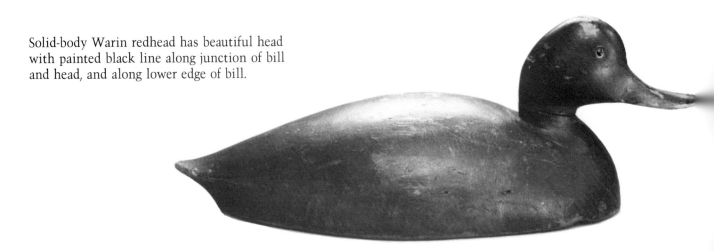

Hollow mallard hen by Warin has interesting
feather painting.

Warin ringneck, solid body, with owner's India
ink signature, "C.H. Gooderham," St. Clair Flats
Company member 1883-95.

Rare Warin greenwing teal with stamp "G.W." on bottom board.

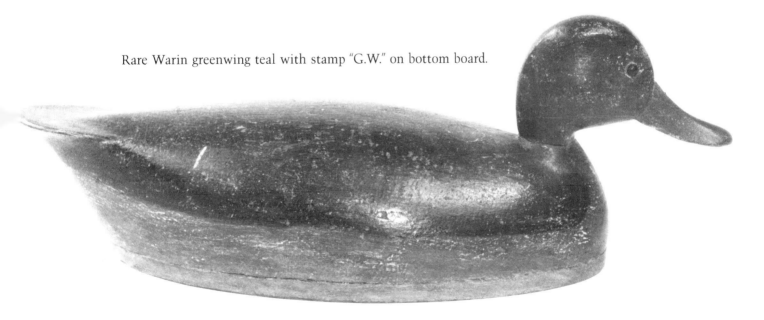

Lowhead black by Warin has the "BUILDERS" stamp.

Standard-size black by Warin has high, hollow
body.

Warin mallard hen with high body.

Cork-body black by John R. Wells.

Mallard with thin bottom board resembling a Warin.

Hollow lowhead black by Wells, c. 1910.

Standard-pose black by Wells.

Canvasback hen by Wells shows flair for feather painting.

Hollow bluebill hen weighing only 14 ounces is at peak of Wells' wide range of quality.

Hollow Wells bluebill drake has unusual round neck, "J.R.W." brand.

Hollow mallard pair has superb painting and head carving similar to George Warin's work. "GOOCH" brand on bottom.

X-ray of David Ward redhead shows use of wire nails, large body cavity to eliminate as much weight as possible.

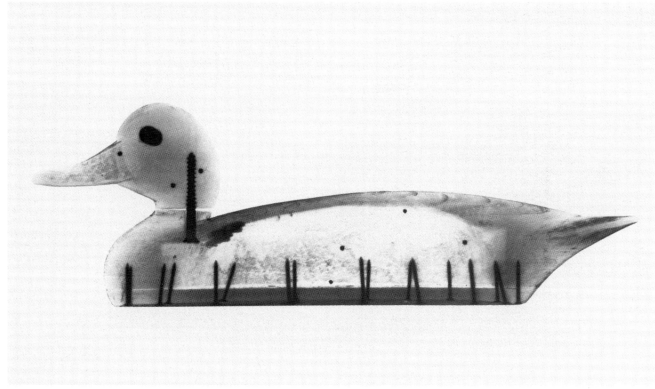

X-ray of mallard drake with "GOOCH" brand shows very thin body shell.

Redhead whose maker was influenced by Stevens factory "humpback" model.

Hen bluebill, front, and hen redhead with striking lines. Redhead is branded "F.B. MENAGH OSHAWA ONT." and "HEM."

Billy Ellis of Whitby turned out this interesting hen pintail.

Goose by David Ward has artistic profile.

Warin goose with ⅜-inch bottom board has pleasing conformation.

Warin goose has spoke-shave marks, ½-inch bottom board.

Solid-body goose by Warin shows same graceful lines as hollow models.

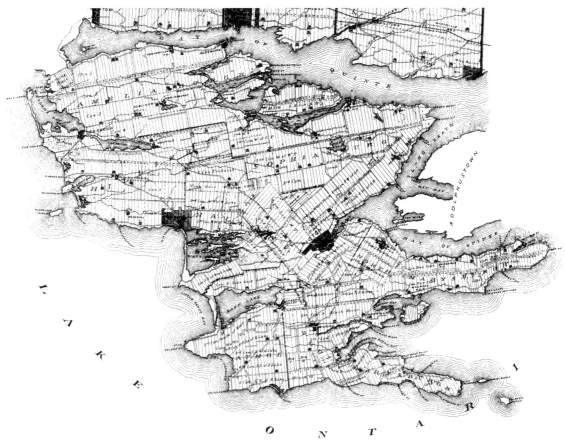

Prince Edward County from Belden's 1878 Historical Atlas.

Hollow black by Charles Melton of Bloomfield has distinctive bulge under tail.

CHAPTER SIX: Prince Edward County

Prince Edward County thrusts southward into eastern Lake Ontario like a jagged jewel, its undulating terrain and hundreds of miles of shoreline providing vistas as breathtaking as the coast of Cornwall. Picture-book villages like Picton, Bloomfield and Wellington could have been transplanted from England. They have a quaint, old-fashioned atmosphere much like that of the land that nurtured Prince Edward.

The Bay of Quinte and dozens of other bays and waterways, lakes and ponds are important stopovers for hundreds of thousands of waterfowl that migrate through the region. Duck hunters and their decoys have been part of the surroundings for at least 140 years and collectors have reaped their rewards ever since Frank Ash, an American, and Laverne Wright of Picton led the parade in the 1940s.

The area for the collector extends a bit beyond Prince Edward County boundaries into such cities as Belleville, Trenton and Brighton, all of which have their contributors to the decoy art.

The Prince Edward decoys, in addition to being hollow and very light, have some unique profiles. Many of the black ducks, for example, have a rounded bulge under their tail, and one time while visiting the late Charles Melton on his farm near Bloomfield, I asked him why that bunion-shaped lump was there. "Because that's what a black duck looks like," he answered simply. Since then, I have taken a closer look at the rear ends of black ducks and have to agree with him.

Charlie made 60 blacks like the one on page 140 and on some of them added another detail at the rear to make them even more realistic, an asterisk under the tail which fulfilled his waggish humor to some degree.

Melton, who was born in England in 1903, made beautiful blacks, bluebills and other species in the 1920s and 1930s using the same pattern as his friend, the famed William H. "Will" Smith of Bloomfield.

Smith, known as the "King" of the market hunters on the Bay of Quinte, turned out decoys from 1920-40. Light of weight and hollow, they have the artistry and balance — and the "bump rump" on the blacks — that are appealing to ducks and collectors alike. Harper Stapleton, a Bloomfield house painter, painted most of Will's decoys. Smith died in 1952.

We probably never will know who originated the distinctive rear-end style on the black duck decoys. Three early carvers who used this style were Sanford Gorsline of Demorestville, a cabinetmaker of the 1870s, John Anderson of Mountain View, who was making decoys from 1850-70, and William Rundle of Bloomfield, active from 1880-1900.

Rundle and his cousin Abraham are responsible for some of the lightest of the hollow lightweights ever set on water. Their bluebills had high backs that tapered down to narrow tails and a ¼-inch bottom board. William tailored his heads with some fine carving, but Abe apparently believed fancy heads were a waste of time and just rounded them off and painted in the eyes.

William marked many of his decoys, either under the bill or on the bottom board, with a scratched-in "W M R." At one point he made a branding iron but got his initials backwards. One decoy has a "Я M W" on the bottom board and a "W M R" brand under the tail. I'll bet that Will, seeing his mistake, re-worked the letters to get at least one brand correct. (A similar snafu was made by William Pulling, a member of the St. Clair Flats Shooting Company. For years I had wondered about the unusual brand of "GNILLUP" on some of the club decoys. Only when I asked Ken MacPherson, a staff member of the

Unusual upswept back on this black was early style of C.W. Chrysler.

Black with skyward-looking pose by Jesse Baker of Trenton, c. 1920.

Archives of Ontario, Toronto, to look up the name did I get the mystery solved. He figured it out immediately. Pulling got his brand backwards.)

Cousin Abe used a brand "A R" under the tip of the tail and another "A R" right next to that on the bottom board.

I had wanted to own a Rundle ever since seeing a photo of one in William Mackey's book *American Bird Decoys*. It finally came about under rather unusual circumstances.

Harold Evans of Watertown, New York, acquired the bluebill, he said, from the estate of a person who had committed suicide. No names are available, and perhaps are not important. However, Evans passed the decoy along rather quickly to Dick Bird in Belleville, Ontario, who, upon hearing that I was looking for a Rundle, didn't hesitate in letting it go. In all fairness, he told me the suicide connection.

Now the decoy is on my shelf and I glance at it occasionally, wondering if possibly it is eyeballing me, too, as it did a couple of previous owners. Most collectors, I reassure my wife, who doesn't want it in the house, may be paranoid, but not suicidal. But if ever I catch that Rundle looking at me before I approach it, I'm going to have to take a long vacation.

The black duck decoys of Prince Edward County have interesting features, the bulge under the tail being a fairly common one. On some of them, however, the back sweeps upward at an angle from the neck to the tip of the tail, as on page 142.

C.W. "Bill" Chrysler of Belleville was an exception when it came to finishing off the exterior of his blacks. Feathers and wing patterns are scratched through a basic coat of rusty brown paint. Head and neck painting is well done, with lateral lines scratched over a light grey background. The mandible cut starts at the cheek with an emphatic triangle and extends toward the bill tip about one inch. Chrysler's black on page 203 is my favorite.

Harry Hitchens of Belleville worked in the same time period as Chrysler, the 1920s and 30s, and his work is almost a duplicate of the Chrysler style, no doubt because they made decoys together. He stamped an "H" under the tail. Chrysler usually branded a "C" on the bottom board.

Another black with interesting lines and slightly cocked head, page 142, was made by Jesse Baker of Trenton, c. 1920.

From Brighton came the two blacks, page 145, that have the "folk art" feeling. The mandible cut is such that they appear to have big lips — "Fat Lips," I call them. The X-ray of the lowhead reveals *three* screws holding head to body. A little bufflehead, page 144, came from the same unknown carver.

On one of my trips to Prince Edward County I had picked up a whistler with a hollow body, several coats of paint and unusual tail carving, made by Ambro Smith of Trenton, a market hunter in the 1870s. A grandson lived in Trenton, I was told, and I tried to locate him for some additional information. The Trenton directory did not list that particular Smith. Rather than call 15 assorted Smiths, I went on through the city, west along the shoreline of the bay. There are a lot of houses and sheds along the shoreline and they aroused my door-knocking instinct, so I turned into the first driveway leading down to the shore, parked the car near a house, and went up to the door. No, the resident said politely, he was not a duck hunter, but his neighbor was one. A few more steps got me over to the neighbor's house.

The neighbor said he had sold most of his decoys a couple of years previous and had kept 25 as an absolute minimum for his own use. Stressing my interest as a collector, I asked if I could see what kind of decoys he was using. Somewhat hesitant, he finally led me to his shed.

There on the shelf were 24 ordinary decoys wrapped up in their anchor lines. The 25th was not so ordinary. It was a hollow bluebill drake with an unusually long, flared tail and squared-off bill that gave it a very distinct appearance (page 206). The initials on the bottom were "J N K." John Kidd, he told me, had hunted ducks along the bay for many years, and if I wanted any further information I could talk to Kidd's son, who worked at Canadian Tire in Trenton. First, I had to liberate the fine old decoy from the flock. Second, go back into Trenton and find John Kidd's son, Norman.

Hollow bufflehead, same unknown
maker as "fat lips" blacks.

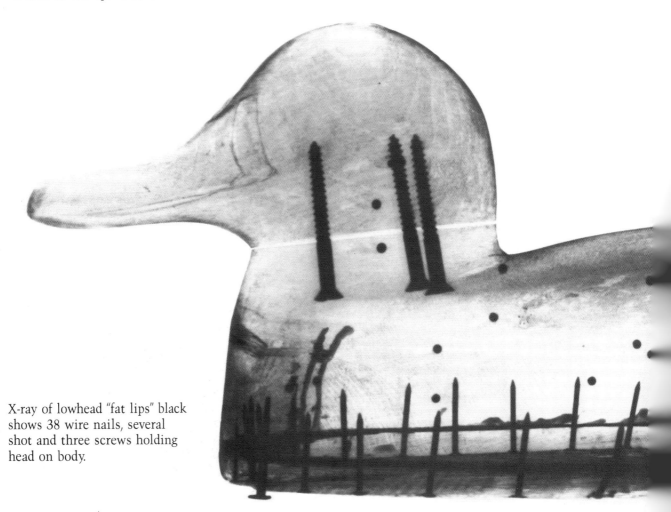

X-ray of lowhead "fat lips" black
shows 38 wire nails, several
shot and three screws holding
head on body.

Pair of hollow blacks with thick mandibles, or "fat lips."

Bluebill by Harve Davern, market hunter
of Brighton, c. 1890.

Dome-back bluebill with hollow body by
Dan Bartlett of West Lake.

Three rare profiles from Picton.

I found him, fortunately, just before his lunch break. He identified the bluebill as having been made by "Beany" Anderson of Trenton in about 1925. "Beany" had copied another local maker, William Andress, who, after making a number of decoys in the 1920s, had moved to Gananoque. If I was interested in this style of decoy, he said, he had some for sale.

We proceeded to his house, inspected several beautiful Anderson canvasbacks on display shelves, then went to the basement, where the sales items were in cardboard boxes.

There were a number of Anderson bluebills, from which I selected the pair on page 205, also a whistler hen, or "brownhead," as they are called in this region. A pair of blue-bills by William Andress did indeed show the similarity of the two makers, the spadetails being a common feature, as seen on page 207. Unlike the hollow bluebill I had found on the bay, they were all solid and with somewhat shorter tails. Visually, they are more interesting seen from above.

Best-known of the Brighton carvers was Harve Davern (1865-1958), a market hunter whose record was 198 bluebills in one day — all the more impressive because he had to load his muzzle-loaders during the hunt. He hunted on Brighton Bay or Wellers Bay, using 45 to 50 decoys, and shipped the ducks to White and Company in Toronto, priced 50 cents to $1.50 a pair, depending on size.

Davern's decoys have a characteristic that make them easily recognizable, a fullness of the throat just under the head, a sort of convex bulge as on page 146 (top).

One of the most prolific of the Prince Edward carvers in the 1920s was Dan Bartlett of West Lake. He made hollow decoys with high, rounded backs that tapered down to a thin little tail about 1½ inches wide and two inches long, as on page 146. Many of these tails did not survive hard usage, and there are few Bartlett decoys left today that have undamaged tails.

The three decoys opposite are a study in profiles. When I found them in Picton, the previous owner offered no clues as to their origin. The bodies are solid and two of them are overpainted in black. The third appears to be in original paint, a black body with white sides that could be an old squaw pattern. The head has some brownish-red paint remaining and what is left of the bill is a bluish-gray. On the bottoms are a poured-in lead weight about ¾ inch in diameter and on one the initials "W V" are cut in. Although the three are badly battle-damaged, they offer interesting silhouettes from the side and above, especially the one with its head pulled back in the resting pose.

The Gorsline clan that lived in the Fish Lake area south of Demorestville produced at least two makers. Howard Gorsline of Marmora said that his grandfather's brother was Sanford Gorsline of the tiny community of Bethel. Sanford was a cabinetmaker who turned out hollow blacks in the 1880s that are attracting collectors' interest.

Sanford's father, George M. Gorssline (an extra "s" was in the name at that time), passed along a hollow black 20 inches long that could have been the first edition of Gorsline waterfowl carpentry. It is in Howard's collection today, given to him by his father.

Howard made some 50 to 75 blacks, mallards, bluebills and whistlers, one of the latter pictured on the next page.

Alert whistler with fold-over wing pattern by Howard Gorsline in the 1950s.

As Prince Edward County and St. Clair Flats decoys are noted for their lightness, I decided one evening to find out what some decoys from those and other areas weighed. Using our kitchen scales, on which each pound is gradated with two-ounce marks, the contest began. I first hauled up from the basement display the products of potential lightweight champion Nate Quillen, who hollowed out even the heads of his lowheads.

The Quillen mallard drake and hen weighed in exactly at 16 ounces each and the widgeon, slightly smaller, hit only 13½ ounces. Six Quillen lowheads gave us some surprising weight differences: 14, 12, 12, 10½, 9 and 9 ounces.

Another couple of trips to the basement and I decided to settle any disputes with the Rundle collectors, who believe that the Rundle, with thin body walls and bottom board, is a flyweight. The Rundle bluebill tipped the scales at 9½ ounces. Very good, but no world record.

A John R. Wells redhead rocked the scales down to 14 ounces, followed by three George Warin redheads, which scored 12, 12 and 11½ ounces.

Four St. Clair Flats bluebill "unknowns" came across the scales at 12, 11, 10 and 10 ounces. Then came a little hollow redhead from the St. Clair Flats Shooting Company. I had to take off a 1½-ounce lead keel before the bird went to the scales. It hit 8½ ounces, the house record!

But wait! I retreated to the basement to see if I had missed any potential candidates. I had. It was a hen bluewing teal (page 100) with the end of its bill broken off and stamped "G.H.R.," for a previous owner, George H. Richards of Boston, a member at the Long Point

Company from 1883-1922. It weighed exactly 8 ounces. (I discounted the tiny fraction of an ounce the missing bill tip would have made.)

And so here, at least, are some lightweight statistics to shoot at. Our house champion — not from the St. Clair Flats, not from Prince Edward County, but from Long Point Bay — awaits challengers.

Like other good duck hunting areas, Prince Edward County has had literally hundreds of excellent decoy makers over the past century. Although many of them are identified by collectors, there are also dozens of unknowns of superior ability. A collector poking around the county gets the added bonus of beautiful scenery — panoramic landscapes and seascapes that can easily turn the trip into a travelogue instead of a decoy expedition. The split rail fences and cedars growing in profusion in the pastures are ornamental counterpoints to the agricultural countryside.

An exposure to Picton is a rewarding one and, if you go there even once, you'll be hooked.

But now, in our meanderings from the St. Clair Flats eastward, we have come to the St. Lawrence River, where we must end this odyssey. It has been an intensely interesting search for the decoy art and makers of long ago. Each decoy reposing on the shelf evokes a memory.

At this particular moment in the evening, I am tired and ready to retire, but one more thing must be settled before I turn in. Doesn't our Charlie Melton black really have that asterisk? I'll go downstairs for a final look.

It's still not there. How could Melton have missed painting in that one naughty detail on this decoy?

As I turn away from the Melton, I glance at the "turtles" — stoics whose ancestry probably will forever confound me. Good night, "turtles."

Then I pause before the "Fat Lips" blacks. I don't really care who made you, Fat Lips, I love you just the same. And that goes for your little brother bufflehead, too.

I look at the "smiling" canvasback and almost return the smile. We used to think it originated in Chatham, but now know it's from Ridgetown, 25 miles farther east. Who cares, Smiley?

The two Glover whistlers, the comics, are worth another pat on their gross wedge-shaped heads, I smile when even I think of them, with their reproachful mien.

I've got one more important thing to check. Turning slowly, so as not to telegraph my intentions, I focus on the suicide Rundle. Was it looking at me? I think not. I will sleep in peace.

As I turn a corner to go upstairs my foot hits a rusty anchor chain attached to a decoy on the floor, back under a shelf. I drag it out. It's a disreputable old canvasback made by the commercial carver Joe Momney of Wallaceburg, Ontario. Many years ago with my sons, Bill and Jon, and daughter, Suzanna, we putt-putted in our outboard to Walpole early in the spring, when the dead marsh grass still was lying flat, for an outing . . . perhaps to cast for pike . . . I forget. Walking along the shore I stumbled over the old canvasback, left there by an Indian guide many years before. You shouldn't be hidden back under a shelf, I tell the old canvasback apologetically. You belong on a pedestal. Because you started it all.

Market hunter Will Smith carved this beautiful black, c. 1920.

Bluebill with high back, painted eyes, branded "AB" for Abraham Rundle, cousin of the famed William Rundle.

X-ray of W. Rundle bluebill shows single screw and washer attaching head, plus tiny wire nails on bottom board.

Bluebill hen by Harry Hitchens of Belleville, c.
1925.

Whistler drake by Harry Hitchens.

Hollow whistler with unusual tail carving by
Ambro Smith, Trenton, c. 1870.

Classic high-head hollow black by J. Althouse of Consecon, who died in 1970 at age 91.

Handsome head rises from narrow breast on hollow black, by Harry Townson of Toronto, c. 1900. "H.T." cut into bottom board, letters ¼-inch high.

Unknown maker bored a hole 8 inches long, 2 inches wide and 1 inch deep in the bottom to lighten decoy. From Belleville area.

Interesting black with 1/4-inch bottom board, tack eyes, flat back, weighing only 14 ounces, by John Anderson, Mountain View, c. 1870.

Upswept back style dominates this large, hollow black with "teeth" showing between mandibles.

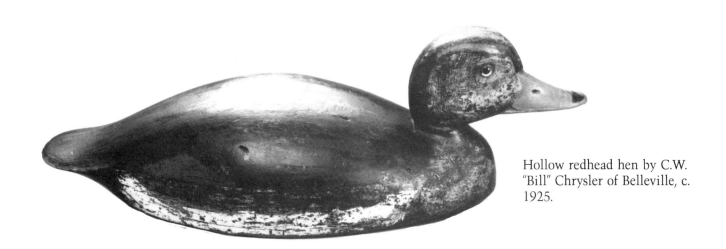

Hollow redhead hen by C.W. "Bill" Chrysler of Belleville, c. 1925.

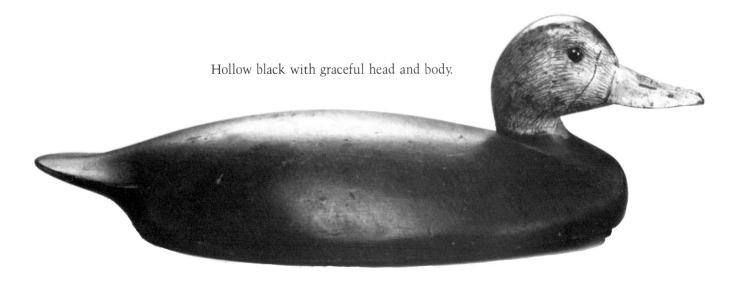

Hollow black with graceful head and body.

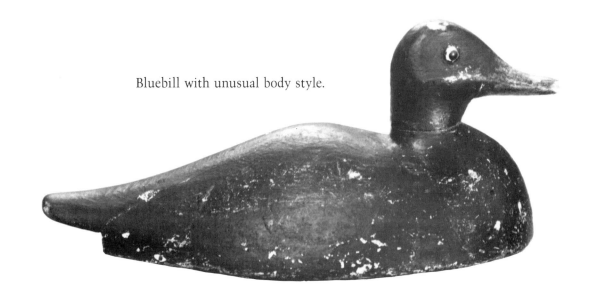

Bluebill with unusual body style.

High-head whistler, alert pose, of Montreal origin.

Whistler with tack eyes, deep mandible cut and wide, solid body.

Whistler hen from Alexandria Bay.

Whistler pair by E.R. "Sprig" Pearson of Kingston.

Hollow whistler by Welland Patterson, Elgin, c. 1950.

Bluebill pair with intriguing profiles by Walter Donaldson of Gananoque.

Hollow redhead with tack eyes by Dan Bartlett.

Whistler hen with wing detail by E.R. "Sprig" Pearson, Kingston.

Bulge under *derriere* is prominent feature of W. Rundle black.

Bluebill of unknown origin has center cut like a Mason Premier.

Sanford Gorsline, who lived near Demorestville, made this charming piece of folk art in the 1880s.

Hollow black with square-cut nails and round holes in bottom board, from George Gorssline rig, c. 1860.

Color Plates

Lowhead greenwing teal by Ted Grace, Walderslade, England.

Alert redhead with flat, hollow body, by Tobin Meldrum.

Canvasback pair by Chris Smith of Algonac, c. 1910.

Rare wood duck by Tom Chambers, c. 1915.

Rare Tom Chambers pintail with graceful head and neck.

The only "known" Chambers whistler, a hollow hen with typical stubby bill.

Aesthetic charm radiates from this long-body Chambers redhead.

Chambers mallard, one of only a few he made late in his career.

Very early Chambers mallard with nice patina, c. 1900.

Chambers canvasbacks with the maker's very best painting.

Short-bodied canvasbacks by Chambers have meticulous painting, stylish flat-top head profiles.

Chambers goose has ½-inch bottom board and body that sweeps up gracefully from neck.

Another Chambers head style for short-body canvasbacks are these rounded-head models.

Chambers made several head styles for redheads, with this rounded-head being his earliest, also most realistic, design.

Redheads with flatter foreheads were a later Chambers style.

Bluebill pair by Chambers, who did not have much demand for the species.

The fine hand of John Schweikart is evident in this impressive pair of whistlers.

Rare American merganser by the Christie brothers of Detroit and Au Gres.

Canvasbacks with unusual profile from the St. Clair Flats Company.

Mallard with pleasing lines, stamped "H G P S" for the Horned Grebe Pleasure Society, a Flats club of the 1950s.

Unusual high-head, folk-arty canvasbacks by Scott Peters, a Potowattimi Indian of Walpole Island, c. 1916.

High-head, hollow canvasback from Harsens Island, the late William Mackey's St. Clair Flats favorite.

Dr. Miles Pirnie carved this handsome mallard pair.

Hooded merganser by Charles Mailloux of Lighthouse Cove, Ontario.

Ferdinand Bach of Detroit made this elegant pair of canvasbacks, c. 1945.

Frank Schmidt black duck has feather stamping, pleasing body contour.

Mallard hen by Frank Schmidt.

Mallard drake by Frank Schmidt retailed through sporting goods store.

Tom Schroeder brant has excellent color shading and water flow-through holes in bottom board, front and rear.

Sleeper canvasbacks made for the St. Anne's Club by William "Bill" Enright of Toledo, Ohio.

Hollow mallard hen with the two halves held together with a long screw from top to bottom, plus machine-cut nails, from Point Mouillee Club, c. 1890.

Lowhead redheads by Nate Quillen, Rockwood, c. 1885.

Quillen widgeon drake with thin bottom board weighs only 13½ ounces.

Pintail pair is perhaps Quillen's most graceful product.

Black by Nate Quillen.

Solid-body bluebill by Quillen sold in the 1880s for 50 cents.

Lowhead redhead by Quillen with "helmut" head style.

Mallard drake on a pintail body is an attractive Quillen combination.

Rare pair of Quillen mallards.

Pintail pair by Jasper Dodge has come through 100-plus years in good original paint.

Peterson or Mason? Rare Barrows golden-eye pair.

Pair of Mason Premier widgeons.

Mason special-order whistler pair with solid, flat bodies, ordered by a Vermont hunter, is only known pair.

Two Premier drakes, one 20 inches long, and a hen, stamped "V.L. & A., Chicago."

Mason Premier pintails with different body styles.

Redhead with tack eyes in indented cheek and fancy painting suggest European origin. Owned by Sir George Drummond, Long Point Company member, 1870.

Charles Reeves' artistry shows in this widgeon with dainty head.

Phineas Reeves mallard has oval-shaped body, a pattern carried on through succeeding Reeves generations.

Canvasback and redhead made of life-preserver cork by Phineas Reeves for James Hewlett.

Mallard pair with hollow bodies and shoe-button eyes, with brand of "ANDREW A. ALLAN" of Montreal, c. 1875.

Unusual old mallard with ½-inch bottom board.

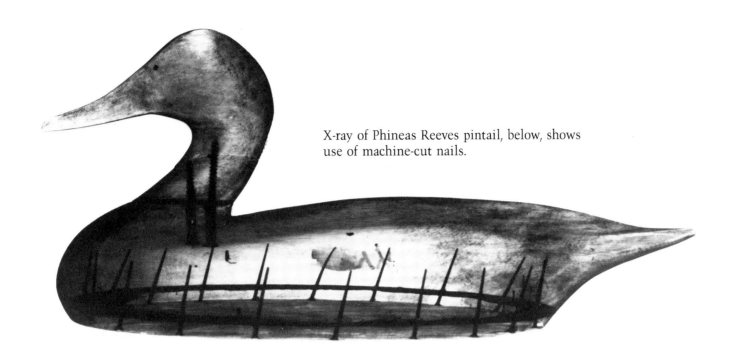

X-ray of Phineas Reeves pintail, below, shows use of machine-cut nails.

Stylish pintail by Phineas Reeves.

Classic pintail with hollow body owned by "D. TISDALE" of Simcoe.

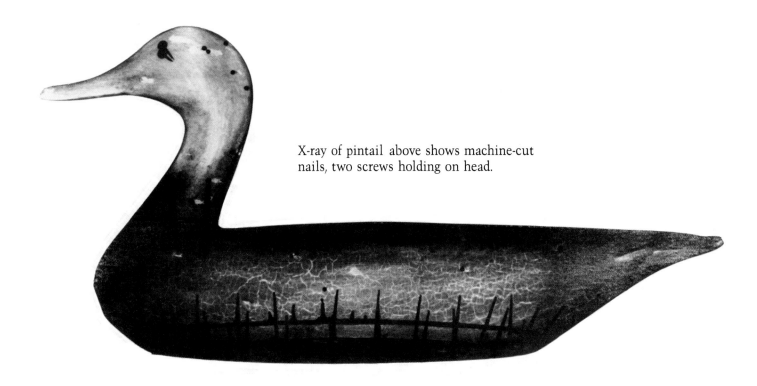

X-ray of pintail above shows machine-cut
nails, two screws holding on head.

Phineas Reeves pintail with flat body style.

Frank Reeves made this canvas-covered pintail, c. 1910.

Bluewing teal from Dr. J.M. Salmon rig, c. 1860.

Charles Reeves liberated his wife's black bead necklace during World War I shortages for this mallard's eyes.

Bluebill pair with subtle shadings and fine rasp work by Peter M. Pringle.

Fine paint combing and good body contour make this bluebill a winner. Has "S. BARKER" stamp, from Big Point Club, Mitchell Bay.

Bluebill by Donny Reid has small peg between neck and body to keep head from turning.

Canvasback by James Barr has regal appearance and peg between neck and body.

Harry Glover made this attractive canvasback, c. 1920.

Glover whistlers have amusing, reproachful look.

Pair of Harry Kretschman bluebills are tiny, hollow birds with hen only nine inches long.

Bluebill pair by Oscar "Oggie" Noorling shows exacting work.

Redhead branded "DALTON MAKER," by Thomas Dalton, has squared-off bill, excellent painting.

Redhead pair with maker "J WEIR" brand also has five owner brands, first of which was "MILLS" for Francis H. Mills of Hamilton, member St. Clair Flats Company, 1879-93.

Canvasback pair by Ivor Fernlund have beautiful sculpture and painting.

Ivor Fernlund redheads have stylish air.

Rare hollow wood duck by Ivor Fernlund is a masterpiece.

Fernlund hollow bluebill drake has good scratch painting.

Hollow redhead by David Ward has good paint combing, weighs only 12 ounces, c. 1880.

George Warin hollow pintail has meticulous painting, his best work.

Warin hollow redhead is a gem.

Bluebill hen by Warin has subtle feathering, painted eyes.

Warin lowhead mallard, an unusual decoy in a period when blacks predominated.

John R. Wells redhead pair with contented, restful look.

Canvasbacks by John Wells are winners of lightweight (15 ounces) canvasback style parade.

Classic pintail pair by John Wells, made for George W. Hendrie, member St. Clair Flats Company 1889-1943.

Hollow redhead by William Ward, Toronto, c. 1880.

W. Rundle bluebill weighs only 9½ ounces.

Bluewing teal with neat and tidy lines.

C.W. Chrysler black has beautiful blend of color and scratch painting.

Interesting bluewing teal.

Hollow canvasback with good combing, from Brighton, c. 1910.

Hollow high-head redhead from Brighton, c. 1910.

Bluebill pair showing spadetail design by Beany Anderson of Trenton.

Bluebill with unusually long spadetail, squared-off bill, by Beany Anderson.

Top view, bluebill by Beany Anderson.

Bluebills by Will Smith of Bloomfield.

Pair of bluebills with good plumage pattern and unusual body style by William Andress of Gananoque.

INDEX